FEAR UNMASKED 2.0

REVISED & UPDATED

Killing the Spirit of Fear, Explaining
the Great Reset, and giving YOU
an Action Plan to Save America

Fear Unmasked 2.0: Killing the Spirit of Fear, Explaining the Great Reset, and Giving YOU an Action Plan to Save America

ISBN 978-1-7364217-5-8

Thrive Publishing

Published by Thrive Publishing
1100 Suite #100 Riverwalk Terrace
Jenks, OK 74037

WHO IS CLAY CLARK?

Clay Clark is the organizer, emcee and host of the Health and Freedom Conferences, and the Reopen America Tour featuring guest speakers including (in no particular order): General Michael Flynn, Lin Wood, Dr. Alan Keyes, Dr. Simone Gold, Roger Stone, Sydney Powell, Jim Caviezel, Pastor Aaron Lewis, Mike Lindell, Sean Feucht, Ann Vandersteel, Pastor Leon Benjamin, Melissa Tate, Pastor Mark Burns, Ian Smith, Dr. Richard Bartlett, Gene Ho, Leigh Dundas, Scott McKay, Dr. Judy Mikovits, Nurse Erin Olzewski, Dr. Scott Jensen, Dr. Christiane Northrup, Dr. Cordie Williams, Charlee Bollinger, Ty Bollinger, Floyd Brown, Joey Gilbert, Sheriff Vic Regalado, Dr. Carrie Madej, Dr. Andy Wakefeld, Sam Sorbo, Pastor Craig Hagin, Jeffrey Prather, Dr. Mark Sherwood, Anna Khait, Leila Centner, Steve Maxwell, Pastor Jackson Lahmeyer, Dr. Rob Marsh, Thomas Renz, Lori Gregory, Del Bigtree, Dr. Sherry Tenpenny, Dr. Eric Nepute, Pastor Greg Locke, Amanda Grace, Jovan Pulitzer, Dr. Shannon Kroner, Patrick Byrne, etc. Clay is, the former "U.S. SBA Entrepreneur of the Year" for the State of Oklahoma, and the host of the Thrivetime Show podcast which has been number one overall on the iTunes business podcast charts 6 times! Clay Clark has also been a member of the Forbes Business Coach Council, and an Amazon best-selling author. Throughout his career Clay's founded several multi-million dollar businesses including: DJConnection.com, EpicPhotos.com, EITRLounge.com, MakeYourLifeEpic.com, etc. (alphabetically speaking). Despite not being a "Deep State Pawn", throughout his career he has been featured in Fast Company, Bloomberg, Forbes, Entrepreneur Magazine, PandoDaily, and numerous other publications. He's been the speaker and consultant of choice for top brands throughout the country including: Hewlett Packard, Maytag University, Valspar Paint, and O'Reilly's Auto Parts. Clay is the co-founder of 5 children, and is the proud owner of thousands of trees, dozens of chickens and 13 cats.

You can download Clay's powerful and practical business books. Visit: www.ThrivetimeShow.com/Free-Resources.

Clay is a business consultant to 160 companies/brands throughout the United States and Canada. You can find his documented client success stories and case studies at: www.ThrivetimeShow.com

Clay's ThrivetimeShow.com podcast which can be listened to without censorship on Rumble.com which has featured interviews with the following guests and more:

PAST INTERVIEWS AND HEADLINES:

> 8x *New York Times* Best-Selling Author and Leadership Expert, **John Maxwell**

> Celebrity Chef, Entrepreneur, and New York Times Best-Selling Author, **Wolfgang Puck**

> Legendary Former Key Apple Employee Turned Venture Capitalist, Best Selling Author, **Guy Kawasaki**

> *New York Times* Best-Selling Co-Author of *Rich Dad Poor Dad*, **Sharon Lechter**

> Senior pastor of the largest church in America with over 100,000 weekly attendees (Lifechurch.tv), **Craig Groeschel**

One of America's most trusted financial experts and has written nine consecutive *New York Times* bestsellers with 7 million+ books in print, **David Bach**

NBA Hall of Famer, **David Robinson** (2-time NBA Champion, 2-time Gold Medal Winner)

Senior Editor for *Forbes* and 3x Best-Selling Author, **Zack O'Malley Greenburg**

Most Downloaded Business Podcaster of All-Time (EOFire.com), **John Lee Dumas**

New York Times Best-Selling Author of *Purple Cow*, and former Yahoo! Vice President of Marketing, **Seth Godin**

Co-Founder of the 700+ Employee Advertising Company (AdRoll), **Adam Berke**

Emmy Award-winning Producer of the *Today Show* and *New York Times* Best-Selling Author of *Sh*tty Moms*, **Mary Ann Zoellner**

New York Times Best-Selling Author of *Contagious: Why Things Catch On* and Wharton Business Professor, **Jonah Berger**

New York Times Best-Selling Author of *Made to Stick* and Duke University Professor, **Dan Heath**

International Best-Selling Author of *In Search of Excellence*, **Tom Peters**

NBA Player and Coach, **Muggsy Bogues** (Shortest player to ever play in the league)

NFL Running Back, **Rashad Jennings** (and Winner of *Dancing with the Stars*)

Lee Cockerell (The former Executive Vice President of Walt Disney World who once managed 40,000 employees)

Michael Levine (PR consultant of choice for Michael Jackson, Prince, Nike, Charlton Heston, Nancy Kerrigan, etc.)

Billboard Contemporary Christian Top 40 Recording Artist, **Colton Dixon**

Conservative Talk Pundint, Frequent *Fox News* Contributor, Political Commentator and Best-Selling Author, **Ben Shapiro**

See additional guests at Thrivetimeshow.com

INTRODUCTION:

This book was written to provide you with the practical guide that you have been praying for to quickly and effectively WAKE UP your friends and family up to the TRUTH related to the COVID-19 Chaos and the mass-scale medical and election fraud that was methodically created to implement Klaus Schwabb's plan called "The Great Reset."

Every statement made in this book is supported by citations, facts, case studies, and irrefutable evidence that can be found at www.TimeToFreeAmerica.com. In previous generations the TRUTH would typically be shared with God-fearing and God-loving people from the pulpit by passionate non-politically correct pastors, but our modern world is now filled with pastors who are more concerned about skinny jeans, fog-machines, and being politically-correct than with sharing the truth. Although my research is not complete, I am fairly certain that Jesus and his apostles did not worry about their 501c3 status when they set out to fulfill the great commission.

LUKE CHAPTER 9: 1-6

¹ Then he called his twelve disciples together, and gave them power and authority over all devils, and to cure diseases.

² And he sent them to preach the kingdom of God, and to heal the sick.

³ And he said unto them, Take nothing for your journey, neither staves, nor scrip, neither bread, neither money; neither have two coats apiece.

⁴ And whatsoever house ye enter into, there abide, and thence depart.

⁵ And whosoever will not receive you, when ye go out of that city, shake off the very dust from your feet for a testimony against them.

⁶ And they departed, and went through the towns, preaching the gospel, and healing everywhere.

CHAPTER 1

WHERE DID THE COVID-19 FEAR ORIGINALLY COME FROM?

THE MODELS THAT PREDICTED THAT 2.2 MILLION AMERICANS WOULD DIE FROM COVID-19 WERE INTENTIONALLY AND NEFARIOUSLY INFLATED BY 25 TIMES.

1.Neil Ferguson's Imperial model could be the most devastating software mistake of all time.

> **Neil Ferguson's Imperial model could be the most devastating software mistake of all time**
>
> The boss of a top software firm asks why the Government failed to get a second opinion from a computer scientist
>
> DAVID RICHARDS AND KONSTANTIN BOUDNIK
> 16 May 2020 - 1:22pm

https://www.telegraph.co.uk/technology/2020/05/16/neil-fergusons-imperial-model-could-devastating-software-mistake/

2.University of Florida Researchers Find No Asymptomatic or Presymptomatic Spread -

> **University of Florida researchers find no asymptomatic or presymptomatic spread**
> *December 22, 2020*

https://alachuachronicle.com/university-of-florida-researchers-find-no-asymptomatic-spread/

3.Who Funded the Abdul Latif Jameel Institute?

https://www.mckinsey.com/business-functions/sustainability/our-insights/how-alj-a-75-year-old-start-up-leads-with-purpose

4.Neil Ferguson Ignored His Own Lockdowns to have an affair with a married women. –

https://www.youtube.com/watch?v=z1GGCqdAlUc&feature=emb_logo

5.Why would Neil Ferguson Recommend Shutting Down America for 12 – 18 months?

https://www.youtube.com/watch?time_continue=1&v=2qKMsGVB_6U&feature=emb_logo

6.LEARN THE TRUTH ABOUT: The False Models, the Inflated Case Numbers and Deaths and the Overhyped Calls for Dangerous Vaccines –

https://www.bitchute.com/video/ EdVxcQsnQQzz/?fbclid=IwARolWN bDossRzbSFEwj-OvdH1nPUBmJ_ yK7HA0wBTFFeDzJvaRkdnZFlsoo

7.Bill Gates is creating these models

https://www.youtube.com/watch?v=9AEMKudv5p0&feature=youtu. be&fbclid=IwAR0T958LlsaKEHQW0AMM_JjilCM_9KEsrCMyehuL_ R5VbcbhxZ5D7gEhbuA – **Watch at 1:52 – 2:50**

8.Was the Model Accurate? 66% of New Coronavirus Cases in New York Are From People Staying at Home – NOT Working or Traveling

https://www.forbes.com/sites/ lisettevoytko/2020/05/06/majority-of- new-coronavirus-cases-in-new-york- are-from-people-staying-at-home-not- traveling-or-working/#77f0752e1655

13

9.Lockdowns of People and Businesses –"Lockdown Was a Waste of Time and Could Kill More Than it Saved, Claims Nobel Laureate Scientist at Stanford University."

Lockdown was a waste of time and could kill more than it saved, claims Nobel laureate scientist at Stanford University

https://www.dailymail.co.uk/news/article-8351649/Lockdown-waste-time-kill-saved-claims-Nobel-laureate.html?fbclid=IwAR1-ie7fCLJD7-Ae–CdTmgbZgnyudqLyFzpHnWEWUuT_M6uv7bST6ph8N4

10.Tens of Thousands of Coronavirus Tests Have Been Double-Counted, Officials Admit

Tens of thousands of coronavirus tests have been double-counted, officials admit

Two samples taken from the same patient are being recorded as two separate tests in the Government's official figures

https://www.telegraph.co.uk/global-health/science-and-disease/tens-thousands-coronavirus-tests-have-double-counted-officials/?fbclid=IwAR0S7D5eisLiLKLNwB_3dcu60GJy17Vv1qqMQTSMgWs5XFr8aJtInin4W4Q

11.According to one Florida County News Team, Hundreds of Coronavirus Deaths Have Been Erroneously Reported and Were Caused by Other Factors.

12.The Loose Guidelines Intentionally Created an Inflated Number of Cases

WHISTLEBLOWING FRONTLINE WORKER ON HOSPITALS BEING PRESSURED TO DRAMATICALLY INFLATE COVID-19 CASES

WATCH

https://www.bitchute.com/video/70Brxd3RDm0W/

13.In 2005, Ferguson Said That Up to 200 million People Could Be Killed from the Bird Flu. In the End, Only 282 People Died Worldwide from the Disease Between 2003 and 2009.
https://www.theguardian.com/ world/2005/sep/30/birdflu.jamessturcke

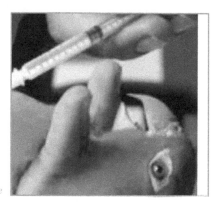

14."It's a Virus That Almost Certainly Will Cause a Global Epidemic," says study author Neil Ferguson,"

Estimates of Future Human Death Toll From Mad Cow Disease Vary Widely

https://www.sciencedaily.com/releases/2009/05/090511151620.htm

15.In 2001 Neil and his team predicted Foot and Mouth Disease Would Create Wide-Spread death. Despite being wrong, his predictions influenced government policy and led to the total culling of more than six million cattle, sheep, and pigs – with a cost to the UK economy estimated at £10 billion.
https://www.telegraph.co.uk/news/2020/03/28/neil-ferguson-scientist-convinced-boris-johnson-uk-coronavirus-lockdown-criticised/

Neil Ferguson, the scientist who convinced Boris Johnson of UK coronavirus lockdown, criticised in past for flawed research

Professor Neil Ferguson predicted Britain was on course to lose 250,000 lives during the coronavirus epidemic

16.In 2002, Ferguson Predicted That Between 50 and 50,000 People Would Likely Die from Exposure to BSE (Mad Cow Disease) in Beef. He also predicted that the number could rise to 150,000 if there was a sheep epidemic as well. In the UK, there have only been 177 deaths from BSE.

Science News	*from research organizations*

Swine Flu Data 'Very Consistent' With Early Stages Of A Pandemic

Date: May 12, 2009
Source: Imperial College London

https://www.nytimes.com/2001/10/30/health/estimates-of-future-human-death-toll-from-mad-cow-disease-vary-widely.html

2 THESSALONIANS 2: 9-12

"9 Even him, whose coming is after the working of Satan with all power and signs and lying wonders, 10 And with all deceivableness of unrighteousness in them that perish; because they received not the love of the truth, that they might be saved. 11 And for this cause God shall send them strong delusion, that they should believe a lie: 12 That they all might be damned who believed not the truth, but had pleasure in unrighteousness."

"If you tell a lie big enough and keep repeating it, people will eventually come to believe it." - Adolf Hilter (One of the worst humans in the history of earth and the Nazi leader who mass murdered thousands of people during and leading up to World War II)

CHAPTER 2

WHAT PERPETUATED THE COVID-19 RELATED FEARS?

THE COVID-19 PCR TESTS WERE FALSELY CALIBRATED TO GROSSLY INFLATE THE NUMBER OF FALSE POSITIVE COVID-19 CASES.

1.WATCH – The Founder of the PCR Kary Mullis Shares – "Tony Fauci doesn't mind going in front of TV and lying on camera. He doesn't understand medicine and he shouldn't be in the position that he is in."

– Kary Mullis (The founder of the PCR test) –

https://www.bitchute.com/ video/55LBX7rj94eZ/

PCR TEST FOUNDER KARY MULLIS SHARES - "TONY FAUCI DOESN'T MIND GOING IN FRONT OF TV AND LYING."

WATCH

02:05

8393   45   0

First published at 13:46 UTC on December 11th, 2020.

Subscribe

ThrivetimeShow
ThrivetimeShow
4860 subscribers

The Founder of the PCR Kary Mullis Shares - "Tony Fauci doesn't mind going in front of TV and lying on camera. He doesn't understand medicine

2.Portuguese Court Rules PCR Tests "Unreliable" &
Quarantines "Unlawful" Important Legal Decision
Faces Total Media Blackout in Western World –

Portuguese Court Rules PCR Tests "Unreliable" & Quarantines "Unlawful"
Important legal decision faces total media blackout in Western world

Tribunal da P...

https://off-guardian.org/2020/11/20/portuguese-court-rules-pcr-tests-unreliable-quarantines-unlawful/

3.Johns Hopkins University Student Newspaper Pulls
Down Article Questioning "COVID-19 Death Tolls."

AMERICA

Johns Hopkins University Newspaper Pulls Down Article Questioning COVID-19 Death Tolls

BY GQ PAN | November 27, 2020 Updated: November 27, 2020   A A   🖶 Print

https://link.theepochtimes.com/mkt_app/johns-hopkins-university-newspaper-pulls-down-article-questioning-covid-19-death-tolls_3595884.html

4. Research for Article Compiled by GENEVIEVE BRIAND

https://web.archive.org/web/20201126163323/

https://www.jhunewsletter.com/article/2020/11/a-closer-look-at-u-s-deaths-due-to-covid-19

5. The Number of Deaths by COVID-19 is Not Alarming. In fact, it has relatively no effect on deaths in the United States. This comes as a shock to many people.

6. How were the number of Covid-19 Deaths Dramatically Inflated? *https://web.archive.org/web/20201126043553/https://www.jhunewsletter.com/article/2020/11/a-closer-look-at-u-s-deaths-due-to-covid-19*

7.WATCH – Senator Doctor Scott Jensen Explains COVID-19 Case Inflation and the Mass-Scale Death Certification Falsification Designed to Inflate COVID-19

8.Is US COVID-19 death count inflated?

https://thehill.com/opinion/healthcare/514915-is-us-covid-19-death-count-inflated

9.US 'Mysteriously' Sees Lowest Flu Season On Record During COVID Pandemic

US 'Mysteriously' Sees Lowest Flu Season On Record During COVID Pandemic

BY TYLER DURDEN   SUNDAY, FEB 28, 2021 - 09:55 AM

https://www.zerohedge.com/covid-19/us-sees-lowest-
flu-season-record-during-covid-pandemic

10. Johns Hopkins University Academic: CDC Data Shows COVID Hasn't Increased US Death Rate

https://www.lifesitenews.com/news/john-hopkins-university-academic-
cdc-data-shows-covid-hasnt-increased-us-death-rate?fbclid=IwAR3diG
CqZjW52c2WZyZ5kaIT32cd_pXPoB3gAi2ivQUFtI-1nMr018zFr9o

11. Johns Hopkins Study, "the number of deaths by COVID-19 is not alarming. In fact, it has relatively no effect on deaths in the United States."

https://pjmedia.com/news-and-
politics/matt-margolis/2020/11/27/
johns-hopkins-study-saying-covid-19-
has-relatively-no-effect-on-deaths-in-
u-s-deleted-after-publication-n1178930

12.The Truth About 2020 Covid-19 Hospitalizations

https://www.coreysdigs.com/health-science/
covid-19-hospitalizations-reality-check/

13.Former Chief Science Officer for Pfizer Says "Second Wave" Faked on False-Positive COVID Tests, "Pandemic is Over"

https://discover.hubpages.com/politics/Pfizer-Chief-Science-Officer-Second-Wave-
Based-on-Fake-Data-of-False-Positives-for-New-Cases-Pandemic-is-Over?fbclid=
IwAR3IypCjPlQn518OToyLO2-VGwneotvxUxT8hYPNBQoOKSSpkqRSFUaI6JI

14.The COVID-19 Testing Fraud Uncovered

https://thehighwire.com/videos/covid-testing-fraud-uncovered/

15.The Centers for Disease Control's COVID-19 Symptoms List is Very Broad to Create More Cases:

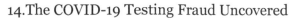

https://www.cdc.gov/coronavirus/2019-ncov/symptoms-testing/symptoms.html

16.Concerns Arise as Some Receive Positive COVID-19 Results But Never Got Tested

*https://www.msn.com/en-us/
Health/medical/concerns-
arise-as-some-receive-positive-
covid-19-results-but-never-
got-tested/ar-BB16Wkwg?oci
d=sf&fbclid=IwAR2f5qoJVJ_
XC_9p3R1SWUmvofEoXnh7wDXh-
ZI8-mk8lcCaZwQa65AQRGI*

17. "Technically Even if You Died of a Clear Alternate Cause, but You Had COVID at the Same Time it is Listed as a COVID Death."

https://www.youtube.com/watch?time_continue=1&v=Tw9Ci2PZKZg&feature=emb_logo

18. "I've Never Received Coaching On How to Do a Death Certificate (Before COVID-19)." – Senator & Dr. Scott Jensen

https://www.youtube.com/watch?time_continue=37&v=PcOJVKfPaXY&feature=emb_logo

19. "The Idea That We Are Going to Allow People to Massage and Game the Numbers is a Real Issue." – Senator Dr. Scott Jensen

https://www.youtube.com/watch?time_continue=1&v=DR2bhCRrYgE&feature=emb_logo

20.Florida Hospital Admits Its COVID Positivity Rate is 10x Lower Than First Reported

https://justthenews.com/politics-policy/coronavirus/florida-lab-admits-its-covid-positivity-rate-was-inflated-90?amp&__twitter_impression=true

21.FDA Investigates Lab as Tens of Thousands of COVID-19 Test Results in Florida Are Questioned

https://www.usatoday.com/story/news/2020/05/21/fda-investigates-microgen-dx-lab-covid-19-test-results-questioned/5222340002/?fbclid=IwAR12K3hsmH16sTTBl-BeXsTOYR-1dIGgdbMxilVW1NQVh-0kMG9QQCULCfQ

22.Florida Hospitals Are Not Reporting Negative Test

Results

https://www.fox2detroit.com/news/fox-35-investigates-florida-department-of-health-says-some-labs-have-not-reported-negative-covid-19-results

23. Covid Testing Kits Are Reporting False Positives

https://www.fda.gov/medical-devices/letters-health-care-providers/false-positive-results-bd-sars-cov-2-reagents-bd-max-system-letter-clinical-laboratory-staff-and

False Positive Results with BD SARS-CoV-2 Reagents for the BD Max System - Letter to Clinical Laboratory Staff and Health Care Providers

f Share   Tweet   Email

The U.S. Food and Drug Administration (FDA) is alerting clinical laboratory staff and health care providers of an increased risk of a false positive result with BD SARS-CoV-2 Reagents for the BD Max System test. In one study, the manufacturer found approximately three percent (3%) of results were false positive results.

24. Orange Country Inflated Case Numbers by Counting Healthy People as Positive

https://www.latimes.com/california/story/2020-07-02/error-led-to-overcount-of-coronavirus-testing-in-orange-county

Los Angeles Times   LOG IN

CALIFORNIA

Orange County inflated its coronavirus test numbers by mistakenly including antibody tests, officials say

25. Florida Fake, False Coronavirus Positives Just Another Reason to Distrust Numbers

MOBILE TESTING FACILITY

Florida fake, false coronavirus positives just another reason to distrust numbers

https://m.washingtontimes.com/news/2020/jul/22/florida-fake-false-coronavirus-positives-just-anot/?fbclid=IwAR3q9dMJLGArgDVyxWfNhxWostmIvvAOwEVe3ReWMPLwW8WKK23R25szhNc

26. New Guidelines Say Coronavirus Antibody Tests Are Pointless

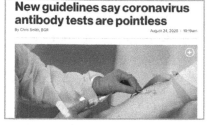

https://nypost.com/2020/08/24/ new-guidelines-say-coronavirus-antibody-tests-are-pointless/

27. This Week CDC Quietly Updated COVID-19 Numbers – Only 9,210 Americans Died From COVID-19 Alone – Rest Had Different Other Serious Illnesses

https://www.cdc.gov/nchs/ nvss/vsrr/covid_weekly/index. htm?fbclid=IwAR2VGGahSK-F4kucO7yd2b6bSmqb3TKw-5FmZDdFjyLD81dLmifNEJKe9BpdU

28. Tennessee Woman Who Died Six Months Ago Receives Letter Last Week Saying She's COVID-19 Positive – *https://www.dailywire. com/news/tennessee-woman-who-died-six-months-ago-receives-letter-last-week-saying-shes-covid-19-positive?utm_source=facebook&utm_medium=social&utm_campaign=b enshapiro&fbclid=IwAR1wvmfZQ m71wilBjAk0AonvAPur-duhRW–r-lCTsWvym4X78Hpnz9x3bw*

29. Did You Know Nashville's Case Numbers in Bars and Restaurants Were SO LOW Officials Emailed Back and Forth About How Best to Hide That Information From the Public, Because They Sill Wanted to Scare People?

https://fox17.com/news/local/covid-19-emails-from-nashville-mayors-office-show-disturbing-revelation

30.Why Would Nashville Hide the Truth from the Public? Emails Reveal Nashville City Government Hid COVID-19 Info From Public to Keep City in Lockdown

https://www.redstate.com/brandon_morse/2020/09/17/nashville-covid-19-lie/

Emails Reveal Nashville City Government Hid COVID-19 Info From Public to Keep City in Lockdown

By Brandon Morse | Sep 17, 2020 11:15 AM ET

31.CDC Compromised by Bias and Conflicts of Interest, Writes Editor of the Journal of American Physicians and Surgeons

CDC Compromised by Bias and Conflicts of Interest, Writes Editor of the Journal of American Physicians and Surgeons

https://www.prnewswire.com/news-releases/cdc-compromised-by-bias-and-conflicts-of-interest-writes-editor-of-the-journal-of-american-physicians-and-surgeons-301134882.html?fbclid=IwAR31jtt8x8JjMOZ-1j4yz8QAN1Zgl5cDHShSa0e65mbdtgDirucZJWVxtkv4

32.”Something Extremely Bogus is Going On. Was Tested for Covid Four Times Today. Two tests came back negative, two came back positive. Same machine, same test, same nurse. Rapid antigen test from BD.”

-Elon Musk

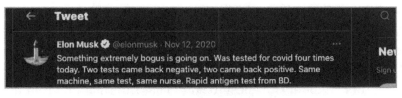

Tweet

Elon Musk @elonmusk · Nov 12, 2020
Something extremely bogus is going on. Was tested for covid four times today. Two tests came back negative, two came back positive. Same machine, same test, same nurse. Rapid antigen test from BD.

https://twitter.com/elonmusk/status/1327125840040169472?s=20

33.WATCH – DR. RICHARD BARTLETT EXPLAINS – THE PCR TESTS INCORRECTLY CALIBRATED TO INFLATE THE NUMBER OF CASES – *https://www. bitchute.com/video/izgHkhV9FMUo/*

34.Portuguese Court Rules PCR Tests "Unreliable" & Quarantines "Unlawful"

https://off-guardian.org/2020/11/20/ portuguese-court-rules-pcr-tests- unreliable-quarantines-unlawful/

35.CDC Report: Officials Knew Coronavirus Test Was Flawed But Released It Anyway

https://www.npr. org/2020/11/06/929078678/cdc- report-officials-knew-coronavirus- test-was-flawed-but-released-it-an yway?fbclid=IwAR1MMXH8 HoLBOJDO4dwPdOC5D2S_ MVPTBUSeoRlnriKoGoQDIc-yFnOpzhg

36. More Evidence Shows Total Deaths in 2020 Are No Different Than Prior Years

https://www.thegatewaypundit.com/2020/12/evidence-shows-total-deaths-

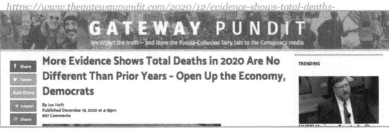

*2020-no-different-prior-years-open-economy-democrats/?fbclid=IwAR1Ay_*
dQQD9U-cv2xEox4rUZ2MfzjHuIUyrzXnFtyBmKYTubgFUhxZknfZw

37. FDA announces that PCR Tests Give False Results.

FDA Admits PCR Tests Give False Results, Prepares Ground For Biden To "Crush" Casedemic

BY TYLER DURDEN   TUESDAY, JAN 05, 2021 - 04:55 AM

The FDA today joined The WHO and Dr.Fauci in admitting there is a **notable risk of false results from the standard PCR-Test** used to define whether an individual is a COVID "Case" or not.

This matters significantly as it fits perfectly with the 'fake rescue' plan we have previously described would occur once the Biden admin took office. But before we get to that 'conspiracy', we need a little background on how the world got here.

https://www.zerohedge.com/covid-19/fda-admits-pcr-tests-give-false-results-
*prepares-ground-biden-virus-rescue-miracle?utm_source=feedburner&utm_*
medium=feed&utm_campaign=Feed%3A+zerohedge%2Ffeed+%28zero+hedge+-+on+a
+long+enough+timeline%2C+the+survival+rate+for+everyone+drops+to+zero%29

38. CDC Skewed CCP Virus Fatalities Higher, Peer-Reviewed Study Claims — *https://www. theepochtimes.com/mkt_app/ peer-reviewed-study-claims- cdc-skewed-ccp-virus-fatalities- upward_3741614.html?v=ul*

A general view of the Centers for Disease Control and Prevention (CDC) headquarters in Atlanta, on Sept. 30, 2014. (Tami Chappell/Reuters)

PUBLIC HEALTH INFORMATION

CDC Skewed CCP Virus Fatalities Higher, Peer-Reviewed Study Claims

BY MARK TAPSCOTT   March 19, 2021 Updated: March 23, 2021   A A 🖶 Print

2 TIMOTHY 1:7

[7] For God hath not given us the spirit of fear; but of power, and of love, and of a sound mind.

CHAPTER 3

DID YOU KNOW THAT COVID-19 IS 100% TREATABLE?

COVID-19 IS EFFECTIVELY AND AFFORDABLY TREATABLE USING IVERMECTIN, BUDESONIDE AND HYDROXYCHLOROQUINE.

1. COVID-19 is 100% Affordably and Effectively Treatable Using Ivermectin, Budesonide and Hydroxychloroquine.

2. Budesonide (Common FDA Approved Asthma Treatment Reduces Need for Hospitalisation for COVID-19)

https://www.ox.ac.uk/news/2021-02-09-common-asthma-treatment-reduces-need-hospitalisation-covid-19-patients-study

3.Doctor Richard Bartlett (MD) Has Successfully Treated 1,000+ COVID-19 Patients with ZERO Deaths - Watch His Newsmax Interview:

https://www.bitchute.com/video/seKC08Nx9fEr/ Read His

Case Study – *http://budesonideworks.com*

4.Who Is Doctor Richard Bartlett (Medical Doctor)? Doctor Bartlett is a former top medical advisor for Texas Governor Rick Perry (for seven consecutive years). Recent Interviews:

> a.Newsmax Interview:
> *https://www.bitchute.com/video/seKC08Nx9fEr/*

> b.One America News:
> *https://www.bitchute.com/video/YKBOfNQqB9CS/*

5.Common Affordable and FDA Approved Asthma Drug Cuts COVID-19 Hospitalization Risk and Recovery Time Read Oxford Study

https://www.reuters.com/article/health-coronavirus-asthma-treatment-int-idUSKBN2A92M7

6.Ivermectin, an FDA-approved, safe, cheap and widely available drug, should be subjected to large-scale trials all over the world to ascertain its effectiveness as pre-exposure prophylaxis for COVID-19.

European Journal of Medical and Health Sciences
www.ejmed.org

Ivermectin as Pre-exposure Prophylaxis for COVID-19 among Healthcare Providers in a Selected Tertiary Hospital in Dhaka – An Observational Study

Mohammed Tarek Alam, Rubaiul Murshed, Pauline Francisca Gomes, Zafor Md. Masud, Sadia Saber, Mainul Alam Chaklader, Fatema Khanam, Monower Hossain, Abdul Basit Ibne Momen, Naz Yasmin, Rafa Faaria Alam, Amrin Sultana, and Rishad Choudhury Robin

https://www.ejmed.org/index.php/ejmed/article/view/599/337

7.FDA Seeks to Stop the Use of Budesonide Drug That Has Successfully Used to Treat Thousands of COVID-19 Patients

https://www.fda.gov/news-events/press-announcements/coronavirus-covid-19-update-daily-roundup-october-2-2020

8.Nebulized Budesonide Improved Oxygenation, Peak, and Plateau Airway Pressures and Significantly Reduced Inflammatory Markers (TNF-α, IL-1β and IL-6) Without Affecting Hemodynamics.

https://www.ncbi.nlm.nih.gov/pmc/articles/PMC5292862/

9. Early Outpatient Treatment Protocol for CoVID-19 Jim Meehan, MD

Dr. Meehan's Early Outpatient Treatment and Prophylaxis Protocols for Viral Illnesses

https://docs.google.com/document/d/1pCf0TRg00G6LFNRzW7V-MzQAH5zyAfX9sNGOUQZqDwA/edit?usp=sharing

10. Doctors cure 6,000 patients with Covid-19 with Ivermectin

https://dominicantoday.com/dr/covid-19/2020/09/29/doctors-cure-6000-patients-with-covid-19-with-ivermectin/

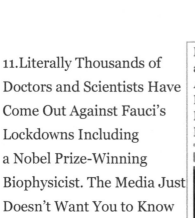

11. Literally Thousands of Doctors and Scientists Have Come Out Against Fauci's Lockdowns Including a Nobel Prize-Winning Biophysicist. The Media Just Doesn't Want You to Know

https://www.redstate.com/michael_thau/2020/07/13/many-medical-experts-were-against-lockdowns-the-media-just-didnt-want-us-know/

12. SHOCKING!!! COVID-19 Is Less Deadly Than the Experts Thought:

- The Infection Fatality Ratio (IFR) parameter has been updated to reflect recently published estimates. This parameter is now presented as the number of deaths per 1,000,000 infections for ease of interpretation.
- The healthcare utilization statistics in Table 2 have been updated to include a 0–17-years-old age group.
- This will be the final update to the COVID-19 Pandemic Planning Scenarios, as there is now a substantial body of published literature that modelers can draw on to inform parameter estimates and assumptions for their models for the general population and for sub-populations of interest. In addition, CDC has several sources that will continue to update COVID-19-related data over time, including COVID Data Tracker, COVID-19 Case Surveillance Public Use Data, and COVID-19-Associated Hospitalization Surveillance Network (COVID-NET).

https://www.cdc.gov/coronavirus/2019-ncov/hcp/planning-scenarios.html

13. "Children Simply Do Not Get Very Sick from This Coronavirus." – Dr. Arthur Reingold (UC Berkeley epidemiologist)

Out of nearly 45,000 confirmed cases in China, only one death in someone younger than 20

https://www.youtube.com/watch?v=Chzu9jGQ6j4&feature=emb_logo

14. Why Are You Just Now Hearing From the Thousands of Doctors Who Successfully Treated COVID-19 Patients?

FRONTLINE DOCTORS ADDRESS THE DISINFORMATION ABOUT COVID-19

https://www.bitchute.com/video/KB5Vh99M8Y5Q/

15. CALIFORNIA CORONAVIRUS SURGE TIED TO INCREASE IN TESTING, NOT REOPENING BUSINESSES, OFFICIAL

https://www.latimes.com/california/story/2020-06-13/california-coronavirus-surge-tied-to-testing-not-reopening-businesses-officials-say

16. "Mounting Evidence Suggests the Coronavirus is More Common and Less Deadly Than it First Appeared."

https://www.npr.org/sections/health-shots/2020/05/28/863944333/antibody-tests-point-to-lower-death-rate-for-the-coronavirus-than-first-thought

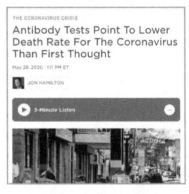

17. School-Age Children More Likely to be Hit by Lighting Than Die of Coronavirus

https://www.telegraph.co.uk/politics/2020/06/09/school-age-children-likely-hit-lightning-die-coronavirus-oxbridge/?fbclid=IwARoCjevkUPW3TFy8i_QPolumu_O-1ratcMUWJxP4I6EHr8EPFa3FFGB-gpw

18.COVID-19 HAS BEEN DANGEROUSLY OVER-HYPED: "For the first time, the CDC has attempted to offer a real estimate of the overall death rate for COVID-19, and under its most likely scenario, the number is 0.26%."

https://www.cdc.gov/coronavirus/2019-ncov/hcp/planning-scenarios.html

19.THE DEATH RATE FOR COVID-19 IS .26%. Florida's Been Open for 2 Months and They Are Thriving *https://www.bitchute. com/video/pqJZgOqfFxfB/?fbclid=IwA R2CdvPA2g-wa054stEsaNL6hUjl474- 6AxtSMnks8TusqI-6-qOliRhQK8*

20.THE COVID-19 NUMBERS ARE BEING massaged:

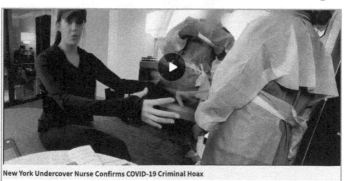

https://banned.video/watch?id=5ee13c3cc7a607002f0c8187&fbclid=IwAR 2d1lKIddGaD4nnDJaOztpPcViWjzZGwdPjLCX-jGXzXLhJSxDqbKF1nu8

21.Trump accuses NYC of Padding Its Coronavirus Death Toll

*https://nypost.com/2020/04/15/
trump-accuses-nyc-of-padding-
its-coronavirus-death-toll/?utm_
source=facebook_sitebuttons&utm_
medium=site+buttons&utm_cam-
paign=site+buttons&fbclid=IwAR0fF-
maiF_3uEovMiZ3QmKnCafc_ly4N-
5Ls_l4uwcabCbp7qL9tuGSOPips*

22.Cases Are Faked

*https://www.dallasnews.com/news/public-health/2020/06/05/some-coronavi-
rus-tests-in-doubt-in-texas-after-lab-turns-up-abnormal-number-of-positives/?fb-
clid=IwAR2HPkOK-AYWZP1OKSqIaaI_04Ns5vqs0iz0sVZJ-53IgEVQZ3edAz4sH2M*

23. United States Centers for Disease Control and Prevention (Scenario 5) is called the "current best estimate" of the parameters of the viral pandemic. That scenario states that the overall fatality rate of infections that show symptoms is around 0.4%. Yet the CDC says it estimates that around 35% of all infectious are asymptomatic, meaning that the total infection fatality rate under the agency's "best estimate" scenario is around 0.26%, or a little more than twice that of the seasonal flu

COVID-19 Pandemic Planning Scenarios

Updated Mar 19, 2021   Print

Summary of Recent Changes

Updates as of March 19, 2021:

- The Infection Fatality Ratio (IFR) parameter has been updated to reflect recently published estimates. This parameter is now presented as the number of deaths per 1,000,000 infections for ease of interpretation.
- The healthcare utilization statistics in Table 2 have been updated to include a 0-17-years-old age group.
- This will be the final update to the COVID-19 Pandemic Planning Scenarios, as there is now a substantial body of published literature that modelers can draw on to inform parameter estimates and assumptions for their models for the general population and for sub-populations of interest. In addition, CDC has several sources that will continue to update COVID-19-related data over time, including COVID Data Tracker, COVID-19 Case Surveillance Public Use Data, and COVID-19-Associated Hospitalization Surveillance Network (COVID-NET).

https://www.cdc.gov/coronavirus/2019-ncov/hcp/planning-scenarios.html

24. The Media Is Focusing On the Number of Cases and Not the Number of Deaths

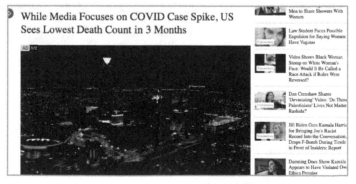

https://www.westernjournal.com/media-focuses-covid-case-spike-us-sees-lowest-death-count-3-months/?utm_source=facebook&utm_medium=huckabee&fbclid=I-wAR24ZWb77AUmypazHEPDpyS3Q5fhMznojVHM1gUS73s8R_5nnERtH48isaE

25.JAPAN ENDS CORONAVI-RUS EMERGENCY WITH 850 DEATHS AND NO LOCKDOWN:

https://www.newsweek.com/japan-ends-coro-navirus-emergency-850-deaths-no-lock-down-1506336?fbclid=IwAR1Lz7uqa-sKpdxV83eVahfd9AOIIDgNeqck4zMk-bYoDUImV7vPT_tyNw_ug

26.Mt. Juliet Man Says Even with No Test, He's Informed He is COVID-19 Positive by the State.

https://www.wsmv.com/news/mt-juliet-man-says-even-with-no-test-he-s-informed-he-is-covid-19/article_f8cf60e6-c886-11ea-8ae0-4ffb48dc9a46.html?utm_medium=social&utm_source=facebook&utm_campaign=user-share&fbclid=IwA R2GlcDNHz03nShOlWDAIzJoKl7TdFw7UqehdhxWLuTQA0bODoVu5NwC14I

27.Public Health England's exaggerated death statistics are a scandal that has fed fear.

https://www.telegraph.co.uk/news/2020/07/17/public-health-englands-exaggerated-death-statistics-scandal/?fbclid=IwAR1eRLFhxdpp8O H2mh6UK5fvvmvPmBEGlnDJM1POLq5DJC6s7yNToNifqj8

28. Sweden's top virologist has a message on how to defeat coronavirus: Open schools and no masks.

HEALTH · CORONAVIRUS

Sweden's top virologist has a message on how to defeat coronavirus: Open schools and no masks

BY BERNHARD WARNER
August 5, 2020 9:00 AM CDT

https://fortune.com/2020/08/05/sweden-anders-tegnell-face-masks-school-opening-coronavirus-covid-19-europe/?fbclid=IwAR1kJkn3vw1lae9xERL86e4rBAMBjj3XRw61eu-HO5e3lnlVakp6NLaQTyA

29. This Week CDC Quietly Updated COVID-19 Numbers – Only 9,210 Americans Died From COVID-19 Alone – Rest Had Different Other Serious Illnesses.

OVID-19 Data from CHS	Weekly Updates by Select Demographic and Geographic Characteristics
ID-19 Death a and Resources	

https://www.cdc.gov/nchs/nvss/vsrr/covid_weekly/index.htm?fbclid=IwAR2VG-GahSKF4kucO7yd2b6bSmqb3TKw5FnZDdFjyLD81dLmifNEJKe9BpdU

JOHN 8:30-33

"30 As he spake these words, many believed on him. 31 Then said Jesus to those Jews which believed on him, If ye continue in my word, then are ye my disciples indeed; 32 And ye shall know the truth, and the truth shall make you free."

CHAPTER 4

CAN YOU TRUST THE CDC?

1.Did You Know That the CDC is Calling in Plain Language for the Implementation of Nazi-Style Concentration Camps To Stop the Spread of COVID-19?

2.Interim Operational Considerations for Implementing the Shielding Approach to Prevent COVID-19 Infections in Humanitarian Settings

> Interim Operational Considerations for Implementing the Shielding Approach to Prevent COVID-19 Infections in Humanitarian Settings
>
> Updated July 26, 2020   Print

https://www.cdc.gov/coronavirus/2019-ncov/global-covid-19/
shielding-approach-humanitarian.html?fbclid=IwAR16k-
HIzASknx8jx49JOhD8Vrrt5E30-g2ipsy19nfSDficm3NFTNf6YmM

JOHN 8:44-45

"44 Ye are of your father the devil, and the lusts
of your father ye will do. He was a murderer from
the beginning, and abode not in the truth, because
there is no truth in him. When he speaketh a lie,
he speaketh of his own: for he is a liar, and the
father of it. 45 And because I tell you the truth,
ye believe me not."

CHAPTER 5

DID YOU KNOW THAT DR. FAUCI FUNDED THE WUHAN LABORATORY AT THE EPICENTER OF THE COVID-19 OUTBREAK?

THE CONTROVERSIAL WUHAN LABORATORY CONDUCTING PANDEMIC-SPREADING GAIN-OF-FUNCTION RESEARCH WAS FOUNDED BY DR. ANTHONY FAUCI

1.Dr. Fauci Backed Controversial Wuhan Lab with U.S. Dollars for Risky Coronavirus Research

https://www.newsweek.com/dr-fauci-backed-controversial-wuhan-lab-millions-us-dollars-risky-coronavirus-research-1500741

2.Watch – Discover the Crimes Against Humanity: Dr. David Martin Shares the Dr. Fauci / COVID-19 Dossier

https://www.bitchute.com/video/XQN9pOwj5BOu/

3.Dr. Fauci Created and Patented the Entire COVID-19 Industrial Complex

https://rumble.com/vea6yj-they-dont-want-us-to-see-this-the-rona-exposed.html

4.Dr. Fauci's Big Lie About Gain-of-Function | The Walls Close in on Fauci & Wuhan

https://rumble.com/vgw41h-episode-939-dr.-faucis-big-lie-the-walls-close-in-on-fauci-and-wuhan.html

5.READ: CONFLICT OF INTEREST: World Health Organization's COVID Investigator Is Recipient Of Chinese Communist Cash, Worked With Wuhan Lab For 18 Years.

https://thenationalpulse.com/exclusive/who-investigators-ccp-covid-ties/

6.Steve Hilton Finds Stunning Covid 19 Connections: 'Specific Activity That Dr. Fauci Funded and It Is Terrifying'

https://www.bizpacreview.com/2021/01/25/steve-hilton-finds-stunning-covid-19-evidence-specific-activity-that-dr-fauci-funded-and-it-is-terrifying-1020943/?fbclid=IwAR0s9DquZKRNjveloz_ifxg5lWISvnbG4QoH9tLA_jO6xMu1D0R4CPCRc5k

7.Bill Gates, Dr. Fauci, The World Health Organization (WHO), and the National Institute of Allergy and Infectious Diseases (NIAID), Are All Openly Working Together to Create a "Global Vaccine" –

> ## Vaccines Collaboration | Bill & Melinda Gates Foundation

https://www.gatesfoundation.org/Media-Center/Press-Releases/2010/12/ Global-Health-Leaders-Launch-Decade-of-Vaccines-Collaboration

8.Dr. Fauci is the Director of the National Institute of Health. 54 Scientists at the National Institute of the Health Were Recently Fired As a Result of Failing to Disclose Their Financial Ties to the Chinese

The National Institutes of Health has been investigating grantees suspected of not disclosing their links to foreign institutions, notably in China.

Fifty-four scientists have lost their jobs as a result of NIH probe into foreign ties

By Jeffrey Mervis | Jun. 12, 2020, 6:10 PM

Some 54 scientists have resigned or been fired as a result of an ongoing investigation by the National Institutes of Health into the failure of NIH grantees to disclose financial ties to foreign governments. For 93% of the 189 scientists whom NIH has investigated to date, China was the source of their undisclosed support.

https://www.sciencemag. org/news/2020/06/fifty-four- scientists-have-lost-their-jobs- result-nih-probe-foreign-ties

9.Thursday's Indictment Charges Zheng with Grant Fraud for Not Disclosing That

Professor charged over scheme to use $4M in US grant money to conduct research for China

A criminal complaint alleges that Song Guo Zheng was a participant in a Chinese Talent Plan, a program established by China to recruit individuals with access to foreign intellectual property

He Was Engaged in a Scheme to Use Approximately $4.1 million in Grants from the National Institutes of Health (NIH) to Help the Chinese government. He Has Been Ordered Held Without Bond Because a Judge Determined He is a Flight Risk.

https://www.foxnews.com/us/professor-charged- scheme-us-grant-money-research-china

10. Why Did Dr. Fauci Fund the Gain of Function Research That Seeks to Increase the Transmissability of a Virus?

https://dailycaller. com/2021/02/19/gain-of-function- research-joe-biden-white-house- national-institutes-of-health- covid-19-coronavirus-china/

11. Fauci Admits to Deceiving the Public About Herd Immunity Because He Wanted More People to Get Vaccinated

https://www.theblaze.com/news/ready-nyt-fauci-admits-to-deceiving-the-public- about-herd-immunity-because-he-wanted-more-people-to-get-vaccinated

12. China's assault on Texas – This Project Threatens US National Security

https://www.foxnews.com/ opinion/china-assault-texas- threatens-national-security-daniel- hoffman?fbclid=IwAR3Zlu6bmN cmDRvWN-QsackthjYnV974bdQ E5pw7kNpsnRZ2slyPHW0Umho

13.Why Won't Dr. Fauci Share His Communications with the World Health Organization? –

https://www.youtube.com/watch?v=sVdIlkjA3mY&t=99s

14."We Know That U.S. Tax Dollars Were Going to the Chinese Government to Fund This Research on Bat Coronaviruses."

https://www.youtube.com/watch?time_
continue=1&v=aDKbzjvrIFM&feature=emb_logo

15.According to Texas Lieutenant Governor Dan Patrick, "We are not out of ICU beds in Texas. We have 7,200 ICU beds available. Of those we have 1,400 used with COVID!" "Fauci said that he is concerned about states like Texas that skipped over certain things. He doesn't know what he is talking about. The only thing that I'm skipping over is listening to him…He has been wrong every time on every issue. I don't need his advice anymore."

https://www.bitchute.com/video/i787k0VHF2Gm/

16.According to Peter Navarro (an Assistant to the President and Director of the Office of Trade and Manufacturing Policy) "Dr. Fauci has a good bedside manner with the public but he has been wrong about everything I have ever interacted with him on." "Now Fauci is saying that a falling mortality rate doesn't matter when it is the single most important statistic to help guide the pace of our economic reopening."

https://www.usatoday.com/story/opinion/todaysdebate/2020/07/14/anthony-fauci-wrong-with-me-peter-navarro-editorials-debates/5439374002/

17. Harvard Professor Indicted After Allegedly Lying About Ties to Wuhan University, Recruitment Plan

https://www.foxnews.com/us/harvard-professor-indicted-alleged-ties-wuhan-university-recruitment

18. Why is Dr. Fauci Saying Hydroxychloroquine <u>Won't</u> Work, But in 2005 the National Institute of Health (That He is in Charge of) Published an Article That Says It, <u>Will</u>?

https://www.ncbi.nlm.nih.gov/pubmed/16115318

19. False Evidence Used to Stop the Use of Hydroxychloroquine

https://www.theguardian.com/world/2020/jun/04/covid-19-lancet-retracts-paper-that-halted-hydroxychloroquine-trials

20. US Intelligence: Head of WHO (Whom Dr. Fauci Communicated Extensively with) Bought by Chinese Government

*https://www.businessinsider.com/
mike-pompeo-who-workd-health-
organisation-tedros-china-2020-7*

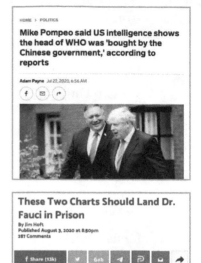

HOME > POLITICS

Mike Pompeo said US intelligence shows the head of WHO was 'bought by the Chinese government,' according to reports

Adam Payne Jul 27, 2020, 6:56 AM

21. These Two Charts Should Land Dr. Fauci in Prison

*https://www.thegatewaypundit.com/2020/08/
two-charts-put-dr-fauci-prison/?utm_source=-
Facebook&utm_medium=PostSideSharing-
Buttons&utm_campaign=websitesharingbut-
tons&fbclid=IwAR34cEAgjk2kbAtY0n_8M8b-
sufep4nCIpoR3yQdsMGslboOoEON0gDrsekg*

These Two Charts Should Land Dr. Fauci in Prison
By Jim Hoft
Published August 3, 2020 at 8:50pm
287 Comments

f Share (13k)　6ab

The **Association of American Physicians and Surgeons (AAPS)** is a leading non-partisan professional association of physicians across the United States.

Today the AAPS filed a motion for a preliminary injunction to compel the release to the public of hydroxychloroquine by the Food & Drug Administration (FDA) and the Department of Health & Human Services (HHS)

22. Why Is Dr. Fauci Losing the Trust of Americans?

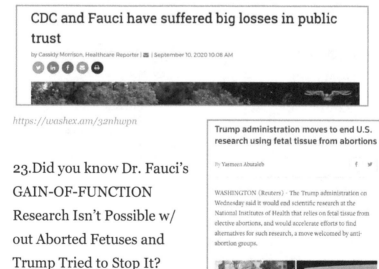

CDC and Fauci have suffered big losses in public trust

by Cassidy Morrison, Healthcare Reporter | ✉ | September 10, 2020 10:08 AM

https://washex.am/32nhwpn

23. Did you know Dr. Fauci's GAIN-OF-FUNCTION Research Isn't Possible w/out Aborted Fetuses and Trump Tried to Stop It?

https://reut.rs/33fcOJp

Trump administration moves to end U.S. research using fetal tissue from abortions

By Yasmeen Abutaleb

WASHINGTON (Reuters) - The Trump administration on Wednesday said it would end scientific research at the National Institutes of Health that relies on fetal tissue from elective abortions, and would accelerate efforts to find alternatives for such research, a move welcomed by anti-abortion groups.

ABORTION

24.Why Did Fauci Move His Gain-Of-Function Research to China?

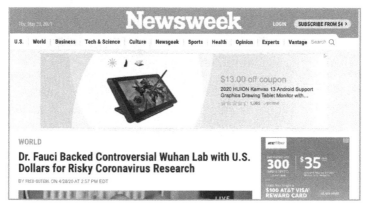

https://bit.ly/3k4U71X

25.What Does It Mean When Fauci Calls for Strengthening WHO, Rebuilding Infrastructure of Human Existence?

https://www.lifesitenews.com/news/
fauci-calls-for-strengthening-who-
rebuilding-infrastructure-of-human-
existence?fbclid=IwAR0u7EMimxw-
*FcmmoGyhzmgU0_*
bdTMGnpuZXpBsPMBLH2h5Dks5-
XADjpm0

26.U.S. State Department Admits COVID-19 Created in Wuhan Lab and Funded by the U.S. Government

https://www.bitchute.com/
video/UtMe248HT4s1/

27.Top World Health Organization official is caught on tape over a year ago revealing that coronavirus manipulation occurring at the Dr. Fauci-funded Wuhan Virology

Lab made it possible to get coronaviruses into human cells using humanized mice models. Watch at 28:10

https://www.bitchute.com/video/R4aiQ1ID8uVz/
https://www.teaparty.org/huge-top-who-official-caught-on-tape-over-a-year-ago-revealing-coronavirus-manipulation-at-wuhan-virology-lab-462319/

28.Fauci Knew About Hydroxychloroquine In 2005 Nobody Needed To Die

https://nw-connection. com/opinion-fauci-knew-about-Hydroxychloroquine-in-2005-nobody-needed-to-die/

JAMES 1:6-10

"[6] But let him ask in faith, nothing wavering. For he that wavereth is like a wave of the sea driven with the wind and tossed. [7] For let not that man think that he shall receive any thing of the Lord. [8] A double minded man is unstable in all his ways. [9] Let the brother of low degree rejoice in that he is exalted:"

CHAPTER 6

DID YOU KNOW THAT WEARING MASKS ACTUALLY MAKES HEALTHY PEOPLE SICK?

1. Dr. Fauci Explains Why Wearing a Mask During a Pandemic is Not Effective

https://www.bitchute.com/video/DtHVePED1PgM/

2. Post-Thanksgiving Mask charts: Still No Evidence That Masks Work

https://rationalground.com/post-thanksgiving-mask-charts-still-no-evidence-that-masks-work/?fbclid=IwAR1iCVaocqITg5MZ-X12hKJvRbMYtRjt_0j9LYO5qyfIeWEQokC2EL07px0

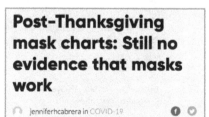

3.Jim Meehan, MD – Wearing Masks Makes Healthy People Sick and Does Not Help to Prevent the Spread of COVID-19

https://www.bitchute.com/ video/FqD95ol67jDE/

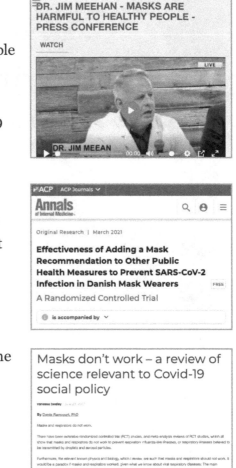

4.Peer-Reviewed Danish Study Finds Masks Don't Protect Wearers From COVID Infection

https://www.acpjournals. org/doi/10.7326/M20-6817

5.America's Frontline Doctors Share Why Mask Mandates Do Not Work

https://www. americasfrontlinedoctors. com/references/#masks

6.Why is Sweden Banning the Wearing of Masks?

COVID Outliers: Why are Swedish Towns Banning Masks?

Outside of Sweden, most Europeans are now used to wearing masks indoors whether in the supermarket, on public transport or when visiting the doctor.

https://nationalinterest.org/blog/reboot/covid-outliers- why-are-swedish-towns-banning-masks-177985

7.YOU WERE PLAYED: Asymptomatic Transmission of COVID-19 Didn't Occur at All, Study of 10 Million Finds

https://thedcpatriot.com/you-were-played-asymptomatic-transmission-of-covid-19-didnt-occur-at-all-study-of-10-million-finds/

YOU WERE PLAYED: Asymptomatic Transmission of COVID-19 Didn't Occur at All, Study of 10 Million Finds

8."We Know That Wearing a Mask Outside Health Care Facilities Offers Little, if Any, Protection from Infection."

https://www.nejm.org/doi/pdf/10.1056/NEJMp2006372?articleTools=true

10.Dr. Jim Meehan, MD Why Healthy People Should Not Wear Masks

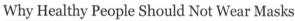

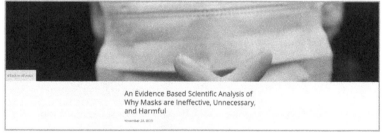

An Evidence Based Scientific Analysis of Why Masks are Ineffective, Unnecessary, and Harmful

https://meehanmd.com/blog/post/173679/an-evidence-based-scientific-analysis-of-why-masks-are-ineffective-unnecessary-and-harmful

11. Effectiveness of Surgical and Cotton Masks in Blocking SARS–CoV-2: A Controlled Comparison in 4 Patients

https://www.acpjournals.org/ doi/10.7326/M20-1342?fbcli d=IwAR1arBfDNIfUrfr1rn4 C44Nuekvob8LbtC94JbCP5 on-TuRlHCm532xwSzU&

12. MIT, Duke, and Medical University of South Carolina graduate Dr. Andrew Kaufman, MD – COVID-19 Tests Meeting FDA Standards Can Be Wrong 50% of theTime

https://www.bitchute.com/ video/V4gEkhSBdy7C/

13. FDA Investigates Lab as Tens of Thousands of COVID-19 Test Results in Florida Are Questioned

– *https://www.usatoday.com/ story/news/2020/05/21/fda- investigates-microgen-dx-lab-covid- 19-test-results-questioned/5222340 002/?fbclid=IwAR12K3hsmH16sTT Bl-BeXsTOYR-1dIGgdbMxilVW1NQVh- okMG9QQCULCfQ*

14. Florida Hospitals Are Not Reporting Negative Test Results

https://www.fox2detroit.com/ news/fox-35-investigates-florida- department-of-health-says- some-labs-have-not-reported- negative-covid-19-results

FOX 35 INVESTIGATES: Florida Department of Health says some labs have not reported negative COVID-19 results

By Robert Guaderrama | Published July 13, 2020 | Updated July 17, 2020 | FOX 35 Orlando

Some Florida labs report 100 percent positivity rates

15. Covid Testing Kits Are Reporting False Positives

https://www.fda.gov/ medical-devices/letters- health-care-providers/ false-positive-results-bd-sars- cov-2-reagents-bd-max-system- letter-clinical-laboratory-staff-and

IN THIS SECTION

← Letters to Health Care Providers

False Positive Results with BD SARS-CoV-2 Reagents for the BD Max System - Letter to Clinical Laboratory Staff and Health Care Providers

f Share ℘ Tweet ✉ Email

The U.S. Food and Drug Administration (FDA) is alerting clinical laboratory staff and health care providers of an increased risk of a false positive result with BD SARS-CoV-2 Reagents for the BD Max System test. In one study, the manufacturer found approximately three percent (3%) of results were false positive results.

Recommendations

The FDA recommends clinical laboratory staff and health care providers:

- Consider any positive result presumptive from tests using the BD SARS-CoV-2 Reagents for the BD Max System. Consider confirming with an alternate authorized test.
- Report any issues with using COVID-19 tests to the FDA. See Reporting Problems to the FDA below.

16. Orange County Inflated Case Numbers by Counting Healthy People as Positive

https://www.latimes.com/ california/story/2020-07-02/error- led-to-overcount-of-coronavirus- testing-in-orange-county

≡   **Los Angeles Times**   LOG IN Q

Orange County inflated its coronavirus test numbers by mistakenly including antibody tests, officials say

17. There is No Medical, Scientific or Constitutional Basis for Mask Mandates State Lab Finds 90 Positive COVID-19 Test Results Were False

State Lab Finds 90 Positive COVID-19 Test Results Were False

7/20/2020

Ninety people who received positive COVID-19 results did not have the virus, according to the state Department of Public Health.

© Provided by NBC Connecticut

The department said the state public health laboratory uncovered a flaw in one of the testing systems it uses to test for SARS-CoV-2, the virus that causes COVID-19, and 90 of 144 people tested between June 15 and July 17 received a false positive

https://www.msn.com/en-us/health/medical/state-lab-finds-90-positive-covid-19-test-results-were-false/ar-BB16Yche?fbclid=IwAR2VrS7VQpL GLJTx_QQ37SpWsqLYDIIvsaSwioWpjp6mZPyPdaX_GZOzy7c

18. Sweden's Health Agency Says Open Schools Did Not Spur Pandemic Spread Among Children –

◇ a.

Sweden's health agency says open schools did not spur pandemic spread among children

By Helena Soderpalm   1 MIN READ

https://www.reuters.com/article/us-health-coronavirus-sweden-schools/swedens-health-agency-says-open-schools-did-not-spur-pandemic-spread-among-children-idUSKCN24G2IS

◇ b.

DOUBLE DUTCH Face masks are 'NOT necessary' and could even harm the fight against coronavirus, say Holland's top scientists

Thomas Burrows

https://www.thesun.co.uk/news/uknews/12292821/face-masks-not-necessary-say-holland-scientists/

19. Is Breathing Air with Less Than 19.5% Oxygen Content Dangerous?

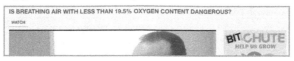

https://www.bitchute.com/video/709AnL03PoFc/

20. The rulemaking record for the Respiratory Protection Standard clearly justifies adopting the requirement that air breathed by employees must have an oxygen content of at least 19.5 percent. A lesser concentration of oxygen in employees' breathing air could endanger them physiologically and diminish their ability to cope with other hazards that may be present in the workplace. The rulemaking record also demonstrates that any workplace atmosphere controlled at or near your recommended minimal oxygen level of 100 mm of mercury at sea level (equivalent to about 13 percent oxygen at sea level) is not safe and healthful for all employees. Exposing employees to partial pressures of oxygen that approach 100 mm of mercury at sea level leaves them with no margin of safety from potentially debilitating effects, which could appear suddenly and without warning.

https://www.osha.gov/laws-regs/standardinterpretations/2007-04-02-0#:~:text=The%20rulemaking%20record%20for%20the,of%20at%20oleast%2019.5%20percen

21.Europe's Top Health Officials Say Masks Aren't Helpful In Beating COVID-19

Europe's Top Health Officials Say Masks Aren't Helpful In Beating COVID-19

AUGUST 6, 2020   NATURAL HEALTH NEWS

https://www.naturalblaze.com/2020/08/europes-top-health-officials-say-masks-arent-helpful-in-beating-covid-19.html?fbclid=IwAR2IDLM6 2xp583SNhkoQosrX2J3RNAX0-y8-1sCvkymH3hHHvs_ffGNtRSs 25.Sweden's top virologist has a message on how to defeat coronavirus: Open schools and no masks

HEALTH · CORONAVIRUS
Sweden's top virologist has a message on how to defeat coronavirus: Open schools and no masks
BY BERNHARD WARNER

https://fortune.com/2020/08/05/sweden-anders-tegnell-face-masks-school-opening-coronavirus-covid-19-europe/?fbclid=IwAR1kJkn3vw 1lae9xERL86e4rBAMBjj3XRw61eu-HO5e3lnlVakp6NLaQTyA

22.Kansas Health Secretary Used Misleading Charts to Push Mask Mandate

Kansas health secretary used misleading charts to push mask mandate
by Madison Dibble, Breaking News Reporter | | August 08, 2020 01:17 PM

https://www.washingtonexaminer.com/news/kansas-health-secretary-used-misleading-charts-to-push-mask-mandate?fbclid=IwAR2pkJIbejV bMRsffs6yA92vJ1w-46mJeu7DCTm5XFeTZ950qHMNmzL-_cU

23.'Don't be a sheep': Washington Sheriff Urges Residents to Defy Mask Order

NEWS
'Don't be a sheep': Washington sheriff urges residents to defy mask order
By Natalie O'Neill   June 25, 2020 | 2:15pm | Updated

https://nypost.com/2020/06/25/ washington-state-sheriff-urges-residents-to-defy-mask-order/?fbclid=IwAR0LndKCSlu3Yek_ ymvOOjRGoBUYjTkMl3UzIGY1PRtzl9Pm23xbZfEb3Ck

24.Oregon Governor Caught Violating Her Own Mask Order

NEWS & POLITICS

Oregon Governor Caught Violating Her Own Mask Order

https://pjmedia.com/news-and-politics/jeff-reynolds/2020/08/07/oregon-governor-and-her-security-detail-caught-violating-mask-order-n751178?fbclid=IwAR2NHUH6Icis59-REPJx-5yTPY68-b6texA3TdqoVjsoutb6qJnEqMEBgkU

25.Dentists say 'Mask Mouth' Can Cause Serious Health Complications, Including Strokes

Dentists say 'mask mouth' can cause serious health complications, including strokes

Sign up for News from Washir Examiner

Email Address

https://www.washingtonexaminer.com/news/mask-mouth-dentists-warn-prolonged-use-of-masks-leading-to-poor-oral-hygiene?fbclid=IwAR1E5th8obDYqJxD9BissBaVLGh1Lp3YRnlKEJRmmSKt3qME5puowdlDFR

26.Pritzker Says Mask Mandate Applies Even While 'Outside and Walking Around'

https://www.nbcchicago.com/news/local/pritzker-says-mask-mandate-applies-even-while-outside-walking-around/2321390/?fbclid=IwAR0Pmay2PzVxqA6TftngRfN3eJ96CtremZaOzLbO4tHN1pwC3Pf2n_QMm24

27. "Europe's Top Health Officials Say Masks Aren't Helpful in Beating COVID-19"

https://www.naturalblaze. com/2020/08/europes- top-health-officials- say-masks-arent-helpful-in-beating-covid-19.html?fbclid=IwAR3N-Qgry0- duDCW02jWU2CP-H_Bk_uCDNkJwXJ5hnethMkqHInNZbNW7As

28. Sweden's Disease Expert Says Just Wearing Face Masks Could Be 'Very Dangerous'

https://nypost. com/2020/08/19/swedens-tegnell-wearing-face-masks-may-be-very-dangerous/

29. 'We See No Point in Wearing a Face Mask,' Sweden's Top Virus Expert Says As He Touts the Country's Improving COVID Numbers

https://fortune.com/2020/07/29/no-point-in-wearing-mask-sweden-covid/?fbclid=Iw AR1I3ttrAFx0x3HetC7D_wS_50Clx7k-xG00HxJ8CtrhVk8m32faqyJWCbk

30. Highly Decorated List of Canadian Doctors Including Two Former Federal Medical Chief Medical Officers Signed an Open Letter Criticizing the Lockdowns and Mask Mandates, etc.

WHO: You Do NOT Need To Wear A Mask

https://principia-scientific.com/who-you-do-not-need-to-wear-a-mask/

31.Healthcare
Professionals Share
– What Are the
Dangers of Mask Mandates?

CLINICAL EVIDENCE & SUPPLEMENTARY DATA

Demonstrating ineffectiveness of masks in surgery

https://themodelhealthshow.com/maskfacts/

32.CDC Guidelines Say Wearing a Mask During
Prolonged Exposure
to Coronavirus Won't
Prevent Possible
Infection

CDC guidelines say wearing a mask during prolonged exposure to coronavirus won't prevent possible infection

https://www.washingtonexaminer.com/news/cdc-guidelines-say-wearing-a-mask-during-prolonged-exposure-to-coronavirus-wont-prevent-possible-infection?fbclid=IwAR3JNCy777N7_bKVrNHRh-VuKbH5JXuYKlOonTV48bgz4tOZt7WxQ9Ujkl2I

33.Have We Been
Lied to About
Masks? What
did the scientific
literature say before
the issue became
political?

https://www.theblaze.com/op-ed/horowitz-lied-to-dramatically-about-masks

Blaze Media / Op-ed

Horowitz: E-MASK-ulation: How we have been lied to so dramatically about masks

What did the scientific literature say before the issue became political?

DANIEL HOROWITZ | September 10, 2020

34. Does Mask Wearing Stop the Spread of COVID-19? No. CDC Study Shows 70% of NEW Coronavirus Cases ALWAYS WORE A MASK, While Only 3.9% NEVER Wore a Mask.

https://www.cdc.gov/mmwr/volumes/69/wr/pdfs/ mm6936a5-H.pdf?fbclid=IwAR2Wi_WEcIZvnh-9ke3w1V MhIxRsAuhoFTsCuDBCROLKuqf1sJx6YUueciA

35. WTH? CDC Admits "At No Time Has CDC Guidance Suggested that Masks Were Intended to Protect the Wearers" (VIDEO)

https://www.thegatewaypundit. com/2020/10/wth- cdc-admits-no-time- cdc-guidance-suggested-masks-intended-protect-wearers-video/

36. The 42 cited pieces of research / data listed below clearly show that masks serve more as instruments of obstruction of normal breathing, rather than as effective barriers to pathogens. Thus, masks should not be mandated / required for the general

public to wear: T Jefferson, M Jones, et al. Physical interventions to interrupt or reduce the spread of respiratory viruses. MedRxiv. 2020 Apr 7.

https://www.medrxiv.org/content/10.1101/2020.03.30.20047217v2

◊   M Walker. Study casts doubt on N95 masks for the public.

≡   MEDPAGE TODAY   ▲

Infectious Disease > Public Health

Study Casts Doubt on N95 Masks for the Public

— Singapore experiment suggests few would wear them correctly, even with instructions

MedPage Today. 2020 May 20.

https://www.medpagetoday.com/infec-tiousdisease/publichealth/86601

◊   C MacIntyre, Q Wang, et al. A cluster randomized clinical trial comparing fit-tested and non-fit-tested N95 respirators to medical masks to prevent respiratory virus infection in health care workers. Influenza J. 2010 Dec 3.

A cluster randomized clinical trial comparing fit-tested and non-fit-tested N95 respirators to medical masks to prevent respiratory virus infection in health care workers

https://onlinelibrary.wiley.com/doi/epdf/10.1111/j.1750-2 659.2011.00198.x?fbclid=IwAR3kRYVYDKb0aR-su9_me9_ vY6a8KVR4HZ17J2A_8of_fXUABRQdhQlc8W0

◊   N Shimasaki, A Okaue, et al. Comparison of the filter efficiency of medical nonwoven fabrics against three different microbe aerosols. Biocontrol Sci. 2018; 23(2). 61-69.

Original

Comparison of the Filter Efficiency of Medical Nonwoven Fabrics against Three Different Microbe Aerosols

NORIKO SHIMASAKI[1*], AKIRA OKAUE[2], RITSUKO KIKUNO[2], AND KATSUAKI SHINOHARA[1]

https://www.jstage.jst.go.jp/article/bio/23/2/23_61/_pdf/-char/en

◇ T Tunevall. Postoperative wound infections and surgical face masks: A controlled study. World J Surg. 1991 May; 15: 383-387.

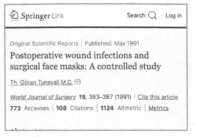

https://link.springer.com/article/10.1007%2FBF01658736

◇ N Orr. Is a mask necessary in the operating theatre? Ann Royal Coll Surg Eng 1981: 63: 390-392.

https://www.ncbi.nlm.nih. gov/pmc/articles/PMC2493952/pdf/annrcse01509-0009.pdf

◇ N Mitchell, S Hunt. Surgical face masks in modern operating rooms – a costly and unnecessary ritual? J Hosp Infection. 18(3); 1991 Jul 1. 239-242.

https://www.journalofhospitalinfection.com/article/0195-6701(91)90148-2/pdf

◇ C DaZhou, P Sivathondan, et al. Unmasking the surgeons: the evidence base behind the use of facemasks in surgery. JR Soc Med. 2015 Jun; 108(6): 223-228.

https://www.ncbi.nlm.nih.gov/pmc/articles/PMC4480558/

◇ L Brosseau, M Sietsema. Commentary: Masks for all for Covid-19 not based on sound data. U Minn Ctr Inf Dis Res Pol. 2020 Apr 1.

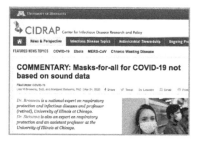

https://www.cidrap.umn.edu/news-perspective/2020/04/commentary-masks-all-covid-19-not-based-sound-data

◇ N Leung, D Chu, et al. Respiratory virus shedding in exhaled breath and efficacy of face masks Nature Research. 2020 Mar 7. 26,676-680 (2020).

RESEARCH ARTICLE
Respiratory Virus Shedding in Exhaled Breath and Efficacy of Face Masks

https://www.researchsquare.com/article/rs-16836/v1

◇ S Rengasamy, B Eimer, et al. Simple respiratory protection – evaluation of the filtration performance of cloth masks and common fabric materials against 20-1000 nm size particles. Ann Occup Hyg.

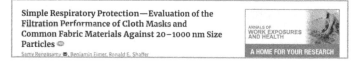

https://academic.oup.com/annweh/article/54/7/789/202744

◇ S Bae, M Kim, et al. Effectiveness of surgical and cotton masks in blocking SARS-CoV-2: A controlled comparison in 4 patients. Ann Int Med. 2020 Apr 6.

Letters | 7 July 2020

Effectiveness of Surgical and Cotton Masks in Blocking SARS–CoV-2: A Controlled Comparison in 4 Patients FREE

⊘ This article has been retracted. See retraction: ∨

Save $100!
Join the ACP Commun

Membership discount expires
May 31, 2021. Use code save2021

https://www.acpjournals.org/doi/10.7326/M20-1342

◇ S Rengasamy, B Eimer, et al. Simple respiratory protection – evaluation of the filtration performance of cloth masks and common fabric materials against 20-1000 nm size particles. Ann Occup Hyg. 2010

https://academic.oup.com/annweh/article/54/7/789/202744

◇ C MacIntyre, H Seale, et al. A cluster randomized trial of cloth masks compared with medical masks in healthcare workers. BMJ Open. 2015; 5(4)

https://bmjopen.bmj.com/content/5/4/e006577.long

◇ W Kellogg. An experimental study of the efficacy of gauze face masks. Am J Pub Health. 1920. 34-42.

https://ajph.aphapublica-tions.org/doi/pdf/10.2105/

AJPH.10.1.34

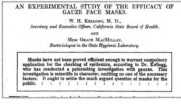

◇ M Klompas, C Morris, et al. Universal masking in hospitals in the Covid-19 era. N Eng J Med. 2020; 382 e63.

Perspective

Universal Masking in Hospitals in the Covid-19 Era

Michael Klompas, M.D., M.P.H., Charles A. Morris, M.D., M.P.H., Julia Sinclair, M.B.A., Madelyn Pearson, D.N.P., R.N.,

https://www.nejm.org/doi/full/10.1056/NEJMp2006372

◊ E Person, C Lemercier et al. Effect of a surgical mask on six minutc walking distance. Rev Mal Respir. 2018 Mar; 35(3):264-268.

> doi: 10.1016/j.rmr.2017.01.010. Epub 2018 Feb 1.
>
> **[Effect of a surgical mask on six minute walking distance]**

https://pubmed.ncbi.nlm.nih.gov/29395560/

◊ B Chandrasekaran, S Fernandes. Exercise with facemask; are we handling a devil's sword – a physiological hypothesis. Med Hypothese. 2020 Jun 22. 144:110002.

> **"Exercise with facemask; Are we handling a devil's sword?" – A physiological hypothesis**
>
> Baskaran Chandrasekaran [1], Shifra Fernandes [2]

https://pubmed.ncbi.nlm.nih.gov/32590322/

◊ P Shuang Ye Tong, A Sugam Kale, et al. Respiratory consequences of N95-type mask usage in pregnant healthcare workers – A controlled clinical study. Antimicrob Resist Infect Control. 2015 Nov 16; 4:48.

> **Respiratory consequences of N95-type Mask usage in pregnant healthcare workers–a controlled clinical study**

https://pubmed.ncbi.nlm.nih.gov/26579222/

◊ T Kao, K Huang, et al. The physiological impact of wearing an N95 mask during hemodialysis as a precaution against SARS in patients with end-stage renal disease. J Formos Med Assoc. 2004 Aug;

> **Respiratory consequences of N95-type Mask usage in pregnant healthcare workers–a controlled clinical study**

https://pubmed.ncbi.nlm.nih.gov/15340662/

◇ F Blachere, W Lindsley et al. Assessment of influenza virus exposure and recovery from contaminated surgical masks and N95 respirators. J Viro Methods.

> **Assessment of influenza virus exposure and recovery from contaminated surgical masks and N95 respirators**

https://pubmed.ncbi.nlm.nih.gov/30029810/

◇ A Rule, O Apau, et al. Healthcare personnel exposure in an emergency department during influenza season. PLoS One. 2018 Aug 31; 13(8): e0203223.

> **Healthcare personnel exposure in an emergency department during influenza season**
>
> Ana M Rule [1], Otis Apau [1], Steven H Ahrenholz [2], Scott E Brueck [2], William G Lindsley [3],

https://pubmed.ncbi.nlm.nih.gov/30169507/

◇ F Blachere, W Lindsley et al. Assessment of influenza virus exposure and recovery from contaminated surgical masks and N95 respirators. J Viro Methods.

> **Assessment of influenza virus exposure and recovery from contaminated surgical masks and N95 respirators**

https://pubmed.ncbi.nlm.nih.gov/30029810/

◇ A Chughtai, S Stelzer-Braid, et al. Contamination by respiratory viruses on our surface of medical masks used by hospital healthcare workers. BMC Infect Dis. 2019 Jun 3; 19(1): 491.

> **Contamination by respiratory viruses on outer surface of medical masks used by hospital healthcare workers**

https://pubmed.ncbi.nlm.nih.gov/31159777/

◇ L Zhiqing, C Yongyun, et al. J Orthop Translat. 2018 Jun 27; 14:57-62.

Surgical masks as source of bacterial contamination during operative procedures

Liu Zhiqing [1], Chang Yongyun [1], Chu Wenxiang [1], Yan Mengning [1], Mao Yuanqing [1],

https://pubmed.ncbi.nlm.nih.gov/30035033/

◇ C MacIntyre, H Seale, et al. A cluster randomized trial of cloth masks compared with medical masks in healthcare workers. BMJ Open. 2015; 5(4)

Research

A cluster randomised trial of cloth masks compared with medical masks in healthcare workers

C Raina MacIntyre [1], Holly Seale [1], Tham Chi Dung [2], Nguyen Tran Hien [2], Phan Thi Nga [2], Abrar Ahmad Chughtai [1],

https://bmjopen.bmj.com/content/5/4/e006577

◇ A Beder, U Buyukko-cak, et al. Preliminary report on surgical mask induced deoxygenation during major surgery. Neurocirugia. 2008; 19: 121-126.

Preliminary report on surgical mask induced deoxygenation during major surgery*

http://scielo.isciii.es/pdf/neuro/v19n2/3.pdf

◇ D Lukashev, B Klebanov, et al. Cutting edge: Hypoxia-inducible factor 1-alpha and its activation-inducible short isoform negatively regulate functions of CD4+ and CD8+ T lymphocytes. J Immunol. 2006

https://www.jimmunol.org/content/177/8/4962

◇ A Sant, A McMichael. Revealing the role of CD4+ T-cells in viral immunity. J Exper Med. 2012 Jun 30; 209(8):1391-1395.

Revealing the role of CD4(+) T cells in viral immunity.

Sant AJ[1], McMichael A

Author information ▸

https://europepmc.org/article/PMC/3420330

37. Do Masks Work? A Danish Controlled Study Says No

https://www.acpjournals.org/doi/10.7326/M20-6817?fbclid=IwAR1tvXvxlCgej8JaDhPVXnhWpF4SUVcaY4SAWCmJ_902lInH2Eoqugf4VE&

Original Research | March 2021

Effectiveness of Adding a Mask Recommendation to Other Public Health Measures to Prevent SARS-CoV-2 Infection in Danish Mask Wearers FREE

A Randomized Controlled Trial

ℹ️ is accompanied by ⌄

Henning Bundgaard, DMSc, Johan Skov Bundgaard, BSc, Daniel Emil Tadeusz Raaschou-Pedersen, BSc, Christian von Buchwald, DMSc, Tobias Todsen, MD,

38. Case for Mask Mandate Rests on Bad Data h

ttps://www.wsj.com/articles/case-for-mask-mandate-rests-on-bad-data-11605113310

OPINION | COMMENTARY

Case for Mask Mandate Rests on Bad Data

A top scientific journal lowballs the percentage of Americans who are already covering their faces.

39. Maker of COVID Tests Says Pandemic is Biggest Hoax Ever Perpetrated

http://www.ini-world-report.org/2020/11/21/maker-of-covid-tests-says-pandemic-is-biggest-hoax-ever-perpetrated/

INI World Report > Big Brother > False Flags > Maker of COVID Tests Says Pandemic is Biggest Hoax Ever Perpetrated

Maker of COVID Tests Says Pandemic is Biggest Hoax Ever Perpetrated

40. Sanford Health CEO steps down after sparking controversy for not wearing mask

Hospitals

Sanford Health CEO steps down after sparking controversy for not wearing mask

https://www.fiercehealthcare.com/hospitals/sanford-health-ceo-steps-down-after-refusing-to-wear-mask?mkt_tok=eyJpIjoiWkdZNVpHWmxNREUwWlRKayIsInQiOiJaUGxhZFwvcUhSdStPa1NETFNYQmtJaVlRaWZzc2RucXZZlwvREdoVk9JMXpHa3QyeGE1RzRWbW95UoR2WGNoSmZwUCtzMGN3TkNTSlNUFdCZTFFUSEJoS3VGMW15dDMwcohxYlFIMjIyVHBGcWRDUO5rVzV2MXhBd2U4RGVhdWdCCIno%3D&mrkid=829978

41. The arguments of the lockdown and mask totalitarians are so fickle that they must resort to unprecedented censorship in order to win the day.

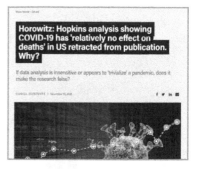

https://www.theblaze.com/
op-ed/horowitz-hopkins-analysis-
showing-covid-19-has-relatively-
no-effect-on-deaths-in-us-retracted

42. German Neurologist Warns Against Wearing Facemasks: 'Oxygen Deprivation Causes Permanent Neurological Damage' (and it's worse for kids) Dr Margarite Griesz-Brisson. AN ABSOLUTELY MUST-READ AND PLEASE SHARE

https://davidicke.com/2020/10/16/
german-neurologist-warns-against-wearing-facemasks-oxygen-deprivation-caus-
es-permanent-neurological-damage-dr-margarite-griesz-brisson/?fbclid=Iw-
AR2e54s8_rGBblJoMMRen3xexbfsuTOWvzN3Estm1iIDj468MzXY2aC33iI

43. Mask Mandates Are Leading To Higher Illness Rates", says OK Health Dept.

https://www.soonerpolitics.org/editorial/mask-mandates-are-
leading-to-higher-illness-rates-says-ok-health-dept

44.Asymptomatic Transmission of COVID-19 Didn't Occur at all, Study of 10 Million Finds

*https://www.lifesitenews.com/news/
asymptomatic-transmission-of-covid-
19-didnt-occur-at-all-study-of-10-
million-finds?fbclid=IwAR0YSwelwFi_
Q7nh6c2wV-brSEBVAIquwTkuV
i6ypUy67WTg7NG8pjqBp8I*

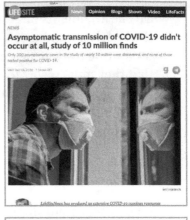

45.Mask Harms in Kids: 68% of Parents Report Alarming Psychological and Physical Problems In First-of-its-kind Study

*https://www.greenmedinfo.com/blog/
mask-harms-kids-68-parents-report-
alarming-problems-first-its-kind-study-
preprint1?utm_campaign=Daily+New
sletter%3A+Mask+Harms+in+Kids%3
A+68%25+of+Parents+Report+Alarm
ing+Psychological+and+Physical+Pro*

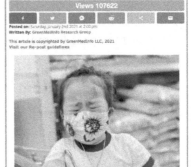

*blems+In+First-of-its-kind+Study+%28UmzESh%29&utm_medium=email&utm_
source=Daily+Newsletter&_ke=eyJrbF9jb21wYW55X2lkIjogIksydlhBeSIsICJrbF9l
bWFpbCI6ICJsZXNaaWVAcmVkZWVtaW5nd2VsbG5lc3MuY29tIn0%3D&fbclid=Iw
AR3rbM-2wJnRpBKv6PnLuDwmPTRBI7PC'sSGnH3nwc2zAob_Z8iHm_gDBwqM*

46.The TRUTH About Facemasks

This article has been retracted.
Retraction in: Med Hypotheses. 2021 May 12; 110601   See also: PMC Retraction Policy

*https://www.ncbi.nlm.nih.gov/pmc/articles/PMC7680614/?fbclid=IwAR0j-
3JN3UFVlIh7YM2VEbrCNiMLXNFeD7I8w8vF2c48YohQ9Ep-3SujM3w*

LUKE 8:17

"[17] For nothing is secret, that shall not be made manifest; neither any thing hid, that shall not be known and come abroad."

CHAPTER 7

SHOULD YOU TRUST THE VACCINES CREATED BY A MAN WHO CHOOSES TO SPEND HIS TIME WITH THE SATANIC, SPIRIT-COOKING, MARINA ABRAMOVIC?

1.Bill Gates' Microsoft Cancels Marina Abramovic Campaign After People Flood Video Calling Her Out As a Satanist

https://newspunch.com/ bill-gates-microsoft-cancel- marina-abramovic-campaign- after-people-flood-video- calling-her-out-satanist/

2.Marina Abramovic Spirit Cooking With Celebreties

PROVERBS 13:20

"He that walketh with wise men shall be wise:
but a companion of fools shall be destroyed."

CHAPTER 8

DID YOU KNOW THAT MICROSOFT ACTUALLY FILED FOR A PATENT WITH A PUBLICATION NUMBER OF WO/2020/060606 FOR A CRYPTO CURRENCY SYSTEM USING BODY ACTIVITY DATA?

1.WO2020060606 - CRYPTOCURRENCY SYSTEM USING BODY ACTIVITY DATA

https://patentscope.wipo.int/search/ en/detail.jsf?docId=WO2020060606

1. WO2020060606 - CRYPTOCURRENCY SYSTEM USING BODY ACTIVITY DATA

Settings

PCT Biblio. Data   Description   Claims   Drawings

ISR/WOSA/A17[2][a]   National Phase   Patent Family

Notices   Documents

2.The Patent Abstract - Human body activity associated with a task provided to a user may be used in a mining process of a cryptocurrency system. A server may provide a task to a device of a user which is communicatively coupled to the server. A sensor communicatively coupled to or comprised in the device of the user may sense body activity of the user. Body activity data may be generated based on the sensed body activity of the user. The cryptocurrency system communicatively coupled to the device of the user may verify if the body activity data satisfies one or more conditions set by the cryptocurrency system, and award cryptocurrency to the user whose body activity data is verified.

REVELATION 13:16-18

"[16] And he causeth all, both small and great, rich and poor, free and bond, to receive a mark in their right hand, or in their foreheads: [17] And that no man might buy or sell, save he that had the mark, or the name of the beast, or the number of his name. [18] Here is wisdom. Let him that hath understanding count the number of the beast: for it is the number of a man; and his number is Six hundred threescore and six."

Human body activity associated with a task provided to a user may be used in a mining process of a cryptocurrency system. A server may provide a task to a device of a user which is communicatively coupled to the server. A sensor communicatively coupled to or comprised in the device of the user may sense body activity of the user. Body activity data may be generated based on the sensed body activity of the user. The cryptocurrency system communicatively coupled to the device of the user may verify if the body activity data satisfies one or more conditions set by the cryptocurrency system, and award cryptocurrency to the user whose body activity data is verified.

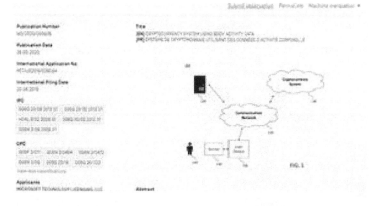

CHAPTER 9

SHOULD YOU TRUST VACCINES CREATED BY A MAN (BILL GATES) WHO CHOSE TO BEFRIEND AND TO INVEST COPIOUS AMOUNTS OF TIME WITH THE WORLD'S MOST PROLIFIC PEDOPHILE (JEFFREY EPSTEIN) AFTER JEFFREY EPSTEIN WAS CONVICTED FOR PEDOPHILIA?

1.Tucker Carlson on the Epstein and Bill Gates Connection

https://www.bitchute.com/video/ IGy0pk1jg57z/?fbclid=IwAR2- ck6OavLVdaL4Fgt6a_NQDAw19SB- ITMhuPXw7HAlWmssUKs265pDpQU

2.Prosecutor in 2009 Epstein Case Said Donald Trump Was the ONLY ONE Who Helped Him

https://www.thegatewaypundit. com/2019/07/prosecutor-in-2009- epstein-case-said-donald-trump-was- the-only-one-who-helped-him/

3.Bill Gates, the Co-Founder of Microsoft Spent a Meaningful Amount of Time with the Sex Offender Jeffrey Epstein, According to Reporting from The *New York Times*. Employees of Gates' Namesake Foundation Reportedly Also Met with Epstein, in Multiple Visits to the Disgraced Financier's Mansion.

Bill Gates Met With Jeffrey Epstein Many Times, Despite His Past

At Jeffrey Epstein's Manhattan mansion in 2011, from left: James E. Staley, at the time a senior JPMorgan executive; former Treasury Secretary Lawrence Summers; Mr. Epstein; Bill Gates, Microsoft's co-founder; and Boris Nikolic, who was the Bill and Melinda Gates Foundation's science adviser.

By Emily Flitter and James B. Stewart

Published Oct. 12, 2019 Updated May 8, 2021

Jeffrey Epstein, the convicted sex offender who committed suicide

https://www.nytimes.com/2019/10/12/business/jeffrey-epstein-bill-gates.html

4.Unlike Many Others, Mr. Gates Started the relationship After Mr. Epstein Was Convicted of Sex Crimes.

◇ 1998: Jeffrey Epstein Purchases Little St. James Island in the U.S. Virgin Islands

◇ May 2006: Charged with multiple counts of unlawful sex acts with a minor

◇ The state attorney at the time, Barry Krischer, referred the case to a grand jury. A grand jury heard from just two of the dozen-plus girls law enforcement had gathered as witnesses, the Miami Heraldreported, and returned an indictment of one count of soliciting prostitution.

◇ 2007: Floats a plea deal with Acosta, the U.S. attorney in Miami at the time

◊   June 2008: Appears in court to plead guilty on two lesser counts and sentenced to a cushy 18 months in jail

◊   Emails obtainedby the Miami Herald show that, during months of back-and-forth negotiations between Epstein's attorneys and Acosta's office, Acosta continually caved to the businessman's demands. Finally, Acosta signed off on a non-prosecution agreement that was "negotiated, signed and sealed so that no one would know the full scope of Epstein's crimes," the Herald stated.

◊   2011 – Beginning in 2011, Mr. Gates met with Mr. Epstein on numerous occasions — including at least three times at Mr. Epstein's palatial Manhattan townhouse: At least once staying late into the night, according to interviews with more than a dozen people familiar with the relationship,

◊   2011: Told to register as a sex offender in New York City - It was later revealed that Epstein never once checked in with the New York Police Department in the eight years since he was told to do so every 90 days in order to verify his address. 2013 – In March 2013, Mr. Gates flew on Mr. Epstein's Gulfstream plane from Teterboro Airport in New Jersey to Palm Beach, Fla., according to a flight manifest. Ms. Arnold said Mr. Gates — who has his own $40 million jet — hadn't been aware it was Mr. Epstein's plane.

◇ 2014 – And in October 2014, Mr. Gates donated $2 million to the Massachusetts Institute of Technology's Media Lab. University officials described the gift in internal emails as having been "directed" by Mr. Epstein. Ms. Arnold said, "There was no intention, nor explicit ask, for the funding to be controlled in any manner by Epstein."

◇ 2017 – At least two senior Gates Foundation officials maintained contacts with Mr. Epstein until late 2017, according to former foundation employees.

◇ 2018: The Miami Herald publishes its exposé on Epstein's long history of alleged sexual abuse

◇ **2020 –** *https://www.newsmax.com/newsfront/ghislaine-max-well-jeffrey-epstein-sex-tapes/2020/07/07/id/976021/*

5.Why Did Bill Gates Say He Had No Relationship with Jeffrey Epstein?

HOME > NEWS

Bill Gates, who said he had no relationship with Jeffrey Epstein, reportedly met with the disgraced financier multiple times, including a 2011 meeting with billionaire Eva Dubin and her teenage daughter

Kat Tenbarge and Meghan Morris   Oct 12, 2019, 5:49 PM

https://www.businessinsider.com/bill-gates-jeffrey-epstein-friendship-swedish-mother-daughter-meeting-2019-10?op=1

6.Jeffrey Epstein Met with Bill Gates to Discuss Philanthropy After He was Jailed for Sex Crimes   *https://nypost.com/2019/08/16/jeffrey-epstein-met-with-bill-gates-to-discuss-philanthropy-after-he-was-jailed-for-sex-crimes-report/*

Jeffrey Epstein met with Bill Gates to discuss philanthropy after he was jailed for sex crimes: report

By Amanda Woods
August 16, 2019 | 10:34am | Updated

7.Why Did Bill Clinton Choose to SpendTime on Epstein's Island?

https://nypost.com/2020/05/26/ clinton-spent-time-on-epsteins- orgy-island-netflix-doc/

Bill Clinton spent time on Jeffrey Epstein's 'orgy island,' Netflix doc says
By Lee Brown
May 26, 2020 | 9:47am | Updated

8.Why Did Bill Clinton Repeatedly Visit Jeffrey Epstein's Orgy Island?

CLINTON CLAIMS Bill Clinton had affair with Jeffrey Epstein 'pimp' Ghislaine Maxwell, according to new book

James Beal, US Editor
27 May 2020, 20:31 | Updated: 28 May 2020, 7:53

https://www.thesun.co.uk/news/11723600/bill-clinton- affair-jeffrey-epstein-pimp-ghislaine-maxwell/

9.Why Is the Arrest of Ghislaine (Guh-LANE) Maxwell so significant?

◇ a.NOTABLE QUOTABLE – "Starting in 1994 until at least 1997, Maxwell had a personal and professional relationship with Jeffrey Epstein." – Audrey Strauss, the acting United State Attorney for the Southern District of New York

◇ b."Maxwell played a critical role in helping Epstein to identify, to befriend and groom minor victims for abuse. In some cases, Maxwell participated in the abuse herself." – Audrey Strauss, the acting United State Attorney for the Southern District of New York

◇ c.Maxwell was the daughter of the late British publishing magnate Robert Maxwell and was the former girlfriend and longtime close associate of Epstein, who killed himself at a federal jail in Manhattan last August while he awaited trial on federal sex trafficking charges.

◇ d.FACT: Maxwell has been indicted on multiple charges, including that she conspired to entice girls as young as 14 to engage in illegal sex acts with Epstein from 1994 through 1997.

TRENDING: ISRAEL | HAMAS | JOE BIDEN | WASHINGTON | CONGRESS | CHINA | DONALD TRUMP | GAZA | MOON JAE | RUSSIA
HOME \ NEWS \ NATIONAL

Ghislaine Maxwell transferred to 'troubled' NYC jail

Follow Us

https://www.washingtontimes.com/news/2020/jul/6/ghislaine-maxwell-jeffrey-epstein-confidante-trans/

◇ e.NOTABLE QUOTABLE – "Several Epstein victims have described Maxwell as his chief enabler, recruiting and grooming young girls for abuse. She has denied wrongdoing and called claims against her "absolute rubbish."

◇ .According to Audrey Strauss, the acting United States Attorney for the Southern District of New York "Maxwell was one of Epstein's closest associates and helped him exploit girls who were as young as 14 years old."

ISAIAH 5:18-20

"20 Woe unto them that call evil good, and good evil; that put darkness for light, and light for darkness; that put bitter for sweet, and sweet for bitter! 21 Woe unto them that are wise in their own eyes, and prudent in their own sight!"

OPENING THE GATES OF HELL

Bill Gates Is Funding The Fear Perpetuating Organization

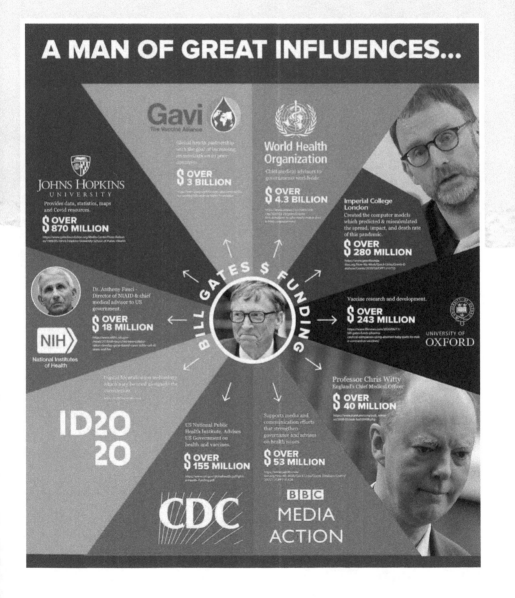

CHAPTER 10

SHOULD YOU TRUST EXPERTS ALL FUNDED BY THE SAME PERSON?

**This verse has been include TWICE to hammer home this point.

ISAIAH 5:18-20

"20 Woe unto them that call evil good, and good evil; that put darkness for light, and light for darkness; that put bitter for sweet, and sweet for bitter! 21 Woe unto them that are wise in their own eyes, and prudent in their own sight!"

CHAPTER 11

DID YOU KNOW THAT THE COVID-19 VACCINES CONTAIN RNA-MODIFYING NANO TECHNOLOGY, BILLIONS OF SPIKED PROTEINS, FETAL-TISSUE CELL LINES, AND THAT MODERNA REFERS TO THEIR VACCINES AS THE "SOFTWARE OF LIFE" AND AS AN "OPERATING SYSTEM"?

1.Doctors Around The World Issue Dire WARNING: DO NOT GET THE COVID VACCINE!

https://api.banned.video/embed/5febc6a8c3c5ce1ce2f5f8d7

2.DR. CHRISTIANE NORTHRUP | WHAT'S INSIDE THE COVID-19 VACCINES?

https://www.thrivetimeshow.com/ business-podcasts/dr-christiane-northrup- whats-inside-the-covid-19-vaccines/

3.No Jab for Me

https://nojabforme.info/

4.What is Actually in the COVID-19 Vaccines?

https://www.
brighteon.com/6bbf3d1b-d9b6-4047-9772-dd277bfe3324

5.Moderna's Description of What Is Inside the COVID-19 Vaccines

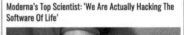

https://www.modernatx.com/mrna-technology/mrna-
platform-enabling-drug-discovery-development

6.Moderna's Top Scientist: 'We Are Actually Hacking The Software Of Life'

https://www.technocracy.
news/modernas-top-
scientist-we-are-actually-
hacking-the-software-of-life/

7.Discover the Horrific Technology Being Developed by the National Institutes of Health - Superparamagnetic nanoparticle delivery of DNA vaccine

https://off-guardian.org/2021/02/15/5-questions-to-ask-
your-friends-who-plan-to-get-the-covid-vaccine/

8.5 questions to Ask Your Friends Who Plan to Get The Covid Vaccine

https://off-guardian.org/2021/02/15/5-questions-to-ask-
your-friends-who-plan-to-get-the-covid-vaccine/

9.Why Is Moderna Modifying Human RNA?

https://www.brighteon. com/f9040036-5a8f-4168- bd95-1f033b4eee78

10.URGENT! 5 Doctors Agree that COVID-19 Injections are Bioweapons and Discuss What to do About It

https://healthimpactnews.com/2021/urgent-5-doctors-agree-that-covid- 19-injections-are-bioweapons-and-discuss-what-to-do-about-it/

11.Johnson & Johnson Covid-19 vaccine: CDC and FDA Recommend US Pause Use of Vaccine Over Blood Clot Concern

https://www.cnn. com/2021/04/13/health/johnson-vaccine-pause-cdc-fda/index.html

12.Learn About the REAL Bill Gates and Why Bill Gates Switched from Microsoft to Vaccines

https://beforeitsnews.com/new-world-order/2021/01/ bill-gates-deleted-documentary-9679.html

13.3 Dozen Cases of Spontaneous Miscarriages, Stillbirths Occurring After COVID-19 Vaccination

https://www.theepochtimes.com/3-dozen-cases-of-spontaneous-miscarriages-stillbirths-occurring-after-covid-19-vaccination_3716385.html

14.What Is In the COVID-19 Vaccines? (with Dr. David Martin and Robert F. Kennedy, Jr.) Watch at 25:46

https://www.bitchute.com/video/eQj2MwpwgTgA/

15. See the COVID-19 Vaccine Adverse Event Reporting System (VAERS)
https://medalerts. org/vaersdb/findfield. php?EVENTS=ON&VAX=COVID19&DIED=Yes

Search Results
From the 5/14/2021 release of VAERS data:
Found 4,201 cases where Vaccine is COVID19 and Patient Died

16. Could Spike Protein in Moderna, Pfizer Vaccines Cause Blood Clots, Brain Inflammation and Heart Attacks?
https://childrenshealthdefense.org/defender/moderna-pfizer-vaccines-blood-clots-brain-inflammation-heart-attacks/

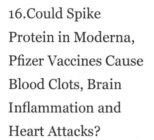

HOME | GENETIC ENGINEERING

Moderna's Top Scientist: 'We Are Actually Hacking The Software Of Life'

17. The New MRNA Vaccines Are Dependency Programs, Designed To Manipulate And Enslave Human Biological Functions – Read How Moderna Explains the Technology
https://humansarefree.com/2021/01/moderna-mrna-jabs-operating-system-program-humans.html

Moderna Admits: MRNA Jabs Are An 'Operating System' Designed To Program Humans

18. January 28th 2021 – Pharmaceutical Company Merck Announced Monday it is Discontinuing Development of its Covid-19 Vaccine Candidates After Early Studies Showed Immune Responses Were Inferior to Natural Infection and other Covid-19 Vaccines

Merck Discontinues Development of SARS-CoV-2/COVID-19 Vaccine Candidates; Continues Development of Two Investigational Therapeutic Candidates

https://www.businesswire.com/news/ home/20210125005234/en/Merck-Discontinues-Development-of-SARS-CoV-2COVID-19-Vaccine-Candidates-Continues-Development-of-Two-Investigational-Therapeutic-Candidates

19. Why Did Microsoft File A Patent For A Crypto Currency System Using Body Activity With A Filing Number Of WO2020060606?

1. WO2020060606 - CRYPTOCURRENCY SYSTEM USING BODY ACTIVITY DATA

PCT Biblio. Data   Description   Claims   Drawings
ISR/WOSA/A17[2][a]   National Phase   Patent Family

https://patentscope.wipo.int/search/en/detail.jsf?docId=WO2020060606

20. Why Did Bill Gates, Dr. Fauci, The World Health Organization (WHO), and the National Institute of Allergy and Infectious Diseases (NIAID), All Decide to Openly Work Together to Create a "Global Vaccine"?

Global Health Leaders Launch Decade of Vaccines Collaboration | Bill & Melinda Gates Foundation

https://www.gatesfoundation.org/Media-Center/Press-Releases/2010/12/
Global-Health-Leaders-Launch-Decade-of-Vaccines-Collaboration

21. Bio-Warfare, Vaccine Danger, & Weaponization of COVID19: Dr. Lee Merrit

URGENT: Bio-Warfare, Vaccine Danger, & Weaponization of COVID19: Dr. Lee Merrit

https://rumble.com/vcvkk9-urgent-bio-warfare-vaccine-danger-
and-weaponization-of-covid19-dr.-lee-merr.html

22. What's in the COVID-19 Vaccines? – 3X *New York Times* Best-selling Author, Dr. Northrup Explains the RNA-MODIFYING CRYPTO-CURRENCY FILLED LUCIFERASE VACCINES

DR. CHRISTIANE NORTHRUP EXPLAINS THE RNA-MODIFYING CRYPTO-CURRENCY FILLED LUCIFERASE VACCINES

WATCH

Epiteliazed dye, delivered along with a vaccine, could enable "on-patient" storage of vaccination history.

BITCHUTE

https://www.bitchute.com/video/6B02k1C1FnlK/

23. Top Medical Inventor: COVID mRNA "Vaccine" Not A Vaccine

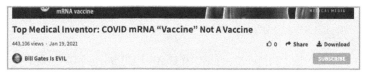

https://cantcensortruth.com/watch?id=60076fda8c03b74ce0e2f6f5

24. 'Perfectly Healthy' Florida Doctor Dies Weeks After Getting Pfizer COVID Vaccine

https://childrenshealthdefense.org/defender/healthy-

florida-doctor-dies-after-pfizer-covid-vaccine/

25. FORCED CHIP WITH A TRACKING DEVICE

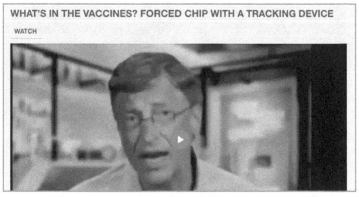

https://www.bitchute.com/video/AC17x0yna01y/

26.Dr. Francis Boyle DARPA's (Defense Advanced
Research Projects Agency) Bio-Warfare Weapon Vaccine
Will Kill People – Watch Now

https://www.bitchute.com/video/p89okxB1AM3B/

27.Head of Pfizer Research: Covid Vaccine is Female
Sterilization

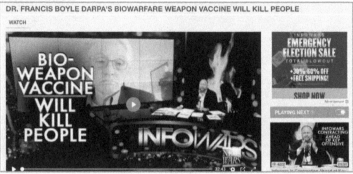

ttps://healthandmoneynews.wordpress.com/2020/12/02/head-
of-pfizer-research-covid-vaccine-is-female-sterilization/

28.Bill Gates is creating these models

https://www.youtube.com/watch?v=9AEMKudv5p0&feature=youtu.
*be&fbclid=IwAR0T958LlsaKEHQW0AMM_JjilCM_9KEsrCMyehuL_*
R5VbcbhxZ5D7gEhbuA

Watch at 1:52 – 2:50

29.Sending Out Contact Tracing Inspectors to Isolate
People

https://truepundit.com/exclusive-bill-gates-negotiated-100-billion-contact-tracing-deal-with-democratic-congressman-sponsor-of-bill-six-months-before-coronavirus-pandemic/

30. Bill Gates Recommends Banning Social Gatherings, Church Services, and the Ability to Dissent Forever Until a "Vaccine" is Given to Everyone

EXCLUSIVE: Bill Gates Negotiated $100 Billion Contact Tracing Deal With Democratic Congressman Sponsor of Bill Six Months BEFORE Coronavirus Pandemic

https://www.youtube.com/watch?v=4X-KkQeMMSQ&t=3s

Watch at 17:20 – 18:04

31. Requiring the User to Do Something is Nothing New for Bill Gates! The United States Versus Bill Gates

https://en.wikipedia.org/wiki/United_States_v._Microsoft_Corp.

32. Bill Gates would be viewed as a criminal if it were not for his investment into Apple in exchange for Steve Jobs' refusal to testify against Bill Gates. Bill Gates Invests $150 million into Apple (the company he almost killed.)

https://www.cnbc.com/2017/08/29/steve-jobs-and-bill-gates-what-happened-when-microsoft-saved-apple.html

33.What is Going On
With Bill Gates During
THIS Deposition?

https://www.youtube.com/
watch?v=jgm455M-N3Y

34. What Is Bill Gates Doing
During THIS Deposition
https://www.youtube.com/

watch?v=gRelVFm7iJE

35.The Only Reason
You Don't Know Bill Gates as a Monopolistic And
Cruel Competition Crushing Entrprenuer is Because

Steve Jobs Needed His Money to Save Apple

https://www.youtube.com/watch?v=I3fBW6XkL34

Watch at :48 seconds

36.The Faux Generosity of the Super-Wealthy: Why Bill
Gates is a Menace to Society

https://www.mintpressnews.com/faux-generosity-how-bill-
gates-bought-his-power-and-influence/263208/

37. The Gates Foundation Donations to the World Health Organization Nearly Match

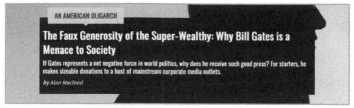

Those from the United States Government

https://www.usnews.com/news/articles/2020-05-29/gates-foundation-donations-to-who-nearly-match-those-from-us-government

38. Bill and Melinda Gates Foundation is Listed As a Member / Partner of the World Health Organization

Gates Foundation Donations to WHO Nearly Match Those From U.S. Government

President Donald Trump announced Friday that the U.S. would be 'terminating' its relationship with the World Health Organization.

By Deidre McPhillips | May 29, 2020, at 4:24 p.m.

Share

https://www.who.int/workforcealliance/members_partners/member_list/gates/en/

39. Why Is the Bill & Melinda Gates Foundation the Largest Non-State Funder of the World Health Organization That Declared COVID-19 as Being a "Pandemic?"

Bill & Melinda Gates Foundation

Member profile

The Bill & Melinda Gates Foundation (Gates) is a funding organization based in Seattle, Washington USA. Guided by the belief that every life has equal value, this innovative group works to help all people lead healthy, productive lives. In partic

https://www.nvic.org/NVIC-Vaccine-News/January-2019/WHO,-Pharma,-Gates.aspx

40. WHAT'S IN THE VACCINES? | LUCIFERASE GENE-LOADED CS-QDOTS AS SELF-ILLUMINATING PROBES

Facebook   Twitter   Pinterest   Email   + More 464   Print   Text Size:

WHO, Pharma, Gates & Government: Who's Calling the Shots?

Posted: 1/27/2019 8:02:52 PM | with 0 comments

https://www.bitchute.com/video/Io5lzbGLUkVU/

41.A Defense Advanced Research Projects Agency (DARPA) -Funded Implantable Biochip To Detect COVID-19 Could Hit Markets By 2021

https://www.zerohedge.com/medical/darpa-funded-implantable-biochip-detect-covid-19-could-hit-markets-2021

WHAT'S IN THE VACCINES? | LUCIFERASE GENE-LOADED CS-QDOTS AS SELF-ILLUMINATING PROBES

WATCH

Transhumanism

42.CDC Admits Vaccines Contain 'Aborted Human Fetus Cells

https://www.thestandardsc.org/baxter-dmitry/cdc-admit-vaccines-contain-aborted-human-fetus-cells

A DARPA-Funded Implantable Markets By 2021

BY TYLER DURDEN

Authored by Raul Diego via MintPressNews.com

43.Biotech Moderna's COVID-19 vaccine investigator leaves FDA advisory committee over conflict of interest

CDC Admits Vaccines Contain 'Aborted Human Fetus Cells'

by The Standard | **Nov 13, 2019** | Baxter Dmitry | 5 comments

https://www.fiercebiotech.com/biotech/moderna-s-covid-vaccine-investigator-leaves-fda-advisory-committee-over-conflict-interest?mkt_tok=eyJpIjoiT-kRjNU9URXhNRE5pTVRNNSIsInQiOiJkckVYUDNwU1JjZllLc1J3bDBqeX-NncDFWamlIenNKdndXbXRJWEIreU5RSoJFcWY1MkVSckVLNTNnVitX-eldSaTA2QTFoNTNLRHdYa2lqRFVocjlJWnRENnR2ZTNOUU13cTFM-V3lhNo1FWGhjS25EbUlUZXRaMTgrVmFFMeEp3NiJ9&mrkid=829978

44.Why Are the COVID-19 Vaccines Filled with RNA-Modifying Cryptocurrency Nano Technology?

Biotech

Moderna's COVID-19 vaccine investigator leaves FDA advisory committee over conflict of interest

by Ben Adams | Sep 24, 2020 7:35am

https://www.bitchute.com/video/6Bo2k1C1Fnl K/

45. Does Injecting an RNA-Modifying, Body-Activated Cryptocurrency with a Patent Number W02020060606 Named Luciferase Into Your Body Sound Like a Good Idea?

https://www.bitchute.com/video/6B02k1C1FnlK/

46. Did you know the Harvard University professor who created the nanotechnology to be included in the RNA-modifying vaccines failed to disclose that he was working with the Chinese?

Harvard University Professor Indicted on False Statement Charges

The former Chair of Harvard University's Chemistry and Chemical

https://www.justice.gov/opa/pr/harvard-university-professor-indicted-false-statement-charges

47. Did you know that Jeffery Epstein was working with Harvard and Bill Gates to Create His Own Race of People Before His Arrests for Pedophelia Related Charges?

https://www.nytimes.com/2019/07/31/business/jeffrey-epstein-eugenics.html

https://www.independent.co.uk/news/world/americas/jeffrey-epstein-seed-human-race-dna-baby-ranch-new-mexico-eugenics-a9030411.html

https://www.theguardian.com/us-news/2019/aug/01/jeffrey-epstein-seed-human-race-report

Jeffrey Epstein Hoped to Seed Human Race With His DNA

By James B. Stewart, Matthew Goldstein and Jessica Silver-Greenberg

July 31, 2019

Epstein reportedly hoped to develop super-race of humans with his DNA

Registered sex offender hoped to seed human race with his DNA by impregnating 20 women at a time, New York Times reports

Jeffrey Epstein 'wanted to seed human race with his DNA' by impregnating up to 20 women at a time, report says

48.

"And that no man might buy or sell, save he that had the mark, or the name of the beast, or the number of his name. Here is wisdom. Let him that hath understanding count the number of the beast: for it is the number of a man; and his number is Six hundred threescore and six."

REVELATION 13:17-18

49.Bamlanivimab for COVID-19 – Guess Who is Investing in the FDA Emergency Authorized Bamlanivimab

Neutralizing Antibodies for COVID-19

https://www.lilly.com/news/media/media-kits/bamlanivimab-covid19

Lilly Announces Arrangement for Supply of Potential COVID-19 Antibody Therapy for Low- and Middle-Income Countries

https://investor.lilly.com/news-releases/news-release-details/lilly-announces-arrangement-supply-potential-covid-19-antibody

50.Former FEMA operative Celeste Solum talks with David Icke: 'The Covid tests are magnetically tagging you and the vaccine is designed for mass depopulation and the synthetic transformation of the human body'

Former FEMA operative Celeste Solum talks with David Icke: 'The Covid tests are magnetically tagging you and the vaccine is designed for mass depopulation and the synthetic transformation of the human body'

294,059 views · Nov 19, 2020   👍 0   ↱ Share   ⬇ Download

https://79days.news/watch?id=5fb6649993b2894247f3c9b4

51. WATCH – Mandatory Vaccines Are The Globalists Hail Mary For Complete Control

Mandatory Vaccines Are The Globalists Hail Mary For Complete Control

14,310 views · Nov 18, 2020   👍 0   ↱ Share   ⬇ Download

http://banned.video/watch?id=5fb5cf2c8cb061413d943955

52. WATCH – AstraZenenca COVID-19 Vaccines Include Lung Tissue from a 14 Month-Old Aborted Male Human Fetus (Baby)

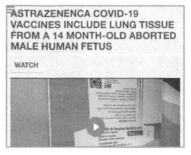

ASTRAZENENCA COVID-19 VACCINES INCLUDE LUNG TISSUE FROM A 14 MONTH-OLD ABORTED MALE HUMAN FETUS

WATCH

https://www.bitchute.com/video/RbOS7ouELtTe/

53. The COVID-19 Vaccines Include MRC-5. What is MRC-5? MRC-5 is a cell line originally developed from the lung tissue of a 14-week-old aborted Caucasian male fetus and you can buy it here

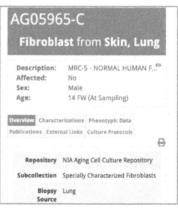

AG05965-C

Fibroblast from **Skin, Lung**

Description: MRC-5 - NORMAL HUMAN F...
Affected: No
Sex: Male
Age: 14 FW (At Sampling)

Overview | Characterizations | Phenotypic Data
Publications | External Links | Culture Protocols

Repository   NIA Aging Cell Culture Repository
Subcollection   Specially Characterized Fibroblasts
Biopsy Source   Lung

https://www.coriell.org/0/Sections/Search/Sample_Detail.aspx?Ref=AG05965-C

54. The Bill Gates, George Soros, and Dr. Fauci Connection Runs Deep – SEE PHOTO (NEXT PAGE)

Fauci Photographed With Soros and Bill Gates' Father, Who Was 'Head of Planned Parenthood'

Bill Gates Made A Stunning Family Revelation

PATRICK HOWLEY · May 31, 2020

https://nationalfile.com/fauci-photographed-with-soros-and-bill-gates-father-who-was-head-of-planned-parenthood/

119

55.How Did Bill Gates Successfully predict when the next pandemic will arrive?

CORONAVIRUS

Bill Gates predicts when the next pandemic will arrive

Covid-19 vaccines developed by Pfizer and BioNTech are awaiting FDA approval but the tech billionaire warns that another virus is inevitable.

https://en.as.com/en/2020/11/24/latest_news/1606228590_532670.html

56.CNN: 'Don't Be Alarmed' if People Start Dying After Taking the Vaccine

Health

CNN: 'Don't Be Alarmed' if People Start Dying After Taking the Vaccine

by Paul Joseph Watson
December 8th 2020, 12:18 pm

https://www.infowars.com/posts/cnn-dont-be-alarmed-if-people-start-dying-after-taking-the-vaccine

57.Two in U.K. Suffer Allergic Reaction to Pfizer's Covid-19 Vaccine Regulator says people with history of significant allergic reactions shouldn't get the shot

> WORLD | EUROPE | U.K.
>
> ## Two in U.K. Suffer Allergic Reaction to Pfizer's Covid-19 Vaccine
>
> Regulator says people with history of significant allergic reactions shouldn't get the shot

https://www.wsj.com/articles/people-with-severe-allergies-shouldnt-get-covid-19-vaccine-says-u-k-regulator-after-reactions-11607515727

58.California bishop warns Catholics not to take COVID vaccine connected in any way to aborted babies

> *NEWS*
>
> ## California bishop warns Catholics not to take COVID vaccine connected in any way to aborted babies
>
> *'If it's using objectionable material, we can't use it, we can't avail ourselves of it,' Fresno Bishop Joseph Brennan stated.*

https://www.lifesitenews.com/news/california-bishop-warns-catholics-not-to-take-covid-vaccine-connected-in-any-way-to-aborted-babies

59. IT'S WAR: Communist China successfully infiltrated vaccine giants Pfizer, AstraZeneca and GlaxoSmithKline as part of "unrestricted warfare" to defeat the US military and conquer North America

https://www.naturalnews.com/2020-12-13-communist-china-infiltrated-vaccine-giants-pfizer-astrazeneca-glaxosmithkline.html

60.EXCLUSIVE: Bill Gates Negotiated $100 Billion Contact Tracing Deal With Democratic Congressman Sponsor of Bill Six Months BEFORE Coronavirus Pandemic

HOMEPAGE, NEWS, POLITICS — JUNE 11, 2020

EXCLUSIVE: Bill Gates Negotiated $100 Billion Contact Tracing Deal With Democratic Congressman Sponsor of Bill Six Months BEFORE Coronavirus Pandemic

https://truepundit.com/exclusive-bill-gates-negotiated-100-billion-contact-tracing-deal-with-democratic-congressman-sponsor-of-bill-six-months-before-coronavirus-pandemic/

61.MSM Targeting Black People With Vaccine Propaganda To Enslave Them

https://79days.news/watch?id=5fdc0d1769a07108b21320a2

62.Founder of Vaccine Safety Website, Ex-Pharma Insider Found Dead

NEWS

Founder of vaccine safety website, ex-pharma insider found dead

'If something were to happen to me,' Brandy Vaughan wrote in late 2019, 'it's foul play and you know exactly who and why.'

https://www.lifesitenews.com/news/founder-of-vaccine-safety-website-ex-pharma-insider-found-dead

63.How Does Abortion, and the Human Fetal Cell Industry Relate to Vaccines

https://avoicefortruth.com/wp-content/uploads/2019/11/White-Paper-Abortion-Human-Fetal-Cell-Industry-Vaccines.pdf

Abortion, the Human Fetal Cell Industry & Vaccines
White Paper

64. "The bill not only permits children of this age (over 11) to provide consent to doctors and other vaccine administrators without a parent's knowledge or consent, but also requires insurance companies, school administrators, and medical personnel to conceal from parents that their child has been vaccinated."

DC passes bill to vaccinate children without parental knowledge, consent

The Minor Consent for Vaccinations Amendment Act permits children as young as 11 'to consent to receive a vaccine,' with all vaccine administrators cooperating to hide the record from parents.

https://www.lifesitenews.com/news/dc-passes-bill-to-vaccinate-children-without-parental-knowledge-consent?fbclid=IwAR2OfEU3gMex4ic3CvZfDWMBf1o_td4VAZNn8TuEpCSRymCjkKXoIl66-LA

65. BILL GATES CAUGHT ON VIDEO ADMITTING VACCINE WILL CHANGE OUR DNA FOREVER

https://www.bitchute.com/video/iKdvO5sxvrDd/

66. CNA Nursing Home Whistleblower: Seniors Are DYING LIKE FLIES After COVID Injections! SPEAK OUT!!!

CNA Nursing Home Whistleblower: Seniors Are DYING LIKE FLIES After COVID Injections! SPEAK OUT!!!

https://healthimpactnews.com/2021/cna-nursing-home-whistleblower-seniors-are-dying-like-flies-after-covid-injections-speak-out/

67. 45-Year-Old Italian Doctor "In the Prime of Life and in Perfect Health" Drops Dead After the Pfizer mRNA COVID Shot: 39-Year-Old Nurse, 42-Year-Old Surgical Technician Also Dead

45-Year-Old Italian Doctor "In the Prime of Life and in Perfect Health" Drops Dead After the Pfizer mRNA COVID Shot: 39-Year-Old Nurse, 42-Year-Old Surgical Technician Also Dead

https://healthimpactnews.com/2021/45-year-old-italian-doctor-in-the-prime-of-life-and-in-perfect-health-drops-dead-after-the-pfizer-mrna-covid-shot-39-year-old-nurse-42-year-old-surgical-technician-also-dead/

68. Watch COVID-19 Vaccine Side-Effects Nurse Develops Bells Palsy Reaction to Pfizer COVID-19 Vaccine

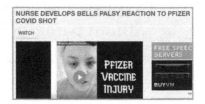

https://www.bitchute.com/video/gofAFCyTH5qg/

69. Side Effects After Receiving Moderna and Pfizer COVID-19 Vaccines

https://www.bitchute.com/video/mL3pwUeQfbnf

70. Nurse Warns America of the Side Effects of COVID-19 Vaccine

Nurse Warns America Of The Side Effects Of COVID-19 Vaccine

https://rumble.com/vc9grd-nurse-warns-america-of-the-side-effects-of-covid-19-vaccine.html

71. "We Just Don't Know the Long-Term Side-Effects of Basically Modifying People's DNA and RNA." – Mark Zuckerberg (Co-Founder of Facebook)

https://t.me/c/1416776839/2888

72. EXC: Bill Gates Foundation Funded Genomics Firm 'Mining' DNA Data Through COVID Tests.

EXC: Bill Gates Foundation Funded Genomics Firm 'Mining' DNA Data Through COVID Tests.

MARCH 8, 2021   NATALIE WINTERS

https://thenationalpulse.com/exclusive/bgi-genomics-gates-foundation-collab/

73. Moderna, J&j, & Pfizer Covid-19 Vaccination: Same Blood Disorders, Cardiac Issues as AstraZeneca

> Moderna, J&j, & Pfizer Covid-19 Vaccination: Same Blood Disorders, Cardiac Issues as AstraZeneca
>
> Updated: Apr 1

https://www.unite4truth.com/post/post-moderna-pfizer-covid-19-vaccination-same-blood-disorder-cardiac-issues-as-astrazeneca

74. Exclusive: Former Pfizer VP to AFLDS: 'Entirely possible this will be used for massive-scale depopulation'

Exclusive: Former Pfizer VP to AFLDS: 'Entirely possible this will be used for massive-scale depopulation'

March 24, 2021

https://www.americasfrontlinedoctors.com/exclusive-former-pfizer-vp-to-aflds-entirely-possible-this-will-be-used-for-massive-scale-depopulation/?utm_source=MadMimi&utm_medium=email&utm_content=Doctors+Uncensored%3A+Bringing+You+The+Truth&utm_campaign=20210406_m162728896_NEWEST+AMY+VERSION+Week+of+4+1+22&utm_term=Read+the+full+article+here

75. Pentagon unveils microchip that senses Covid in the body

Pentagon unveils sensor that detects Covid in the body

https://www.independent.co.uk/news/world/americas/
pentagon-covid-microchip-blood-virus-b1830372.html

NOTABLE QUOTABLE

- DANIEL 2:31-45 - 31

NOTE: Clay is in reference to humanity. Iron is in reference to machines.

"You, O king, were watching; and behold, a great image! This great image, whose splendor was excellent, stood before you; and its form was awesome. [32] This image's head was of fine gold, its chest and arms of silver, its belly and [a]thighs of bronze, [33] its legs of iron, its feet partly of iron and partly of [b]clay. [34] You watched while a stone was cut out without hands, which struck the image on its feet of iron and clay, and broke them in pieces. [35] Then the iron, the clay, the bronze, the silver, and the gold were crushed together, and became like chaff from the summer threshing floors; the wind carried them away so that no trace of them was found. And the stone that struck the image became a great mountain and filled the whole earth. [36] "This is the dream. Now we will tell the interpretation of it before the king. [37] You, O king, are a king of kings. For the God of heaven has given you a kingdom, power, strength, and glory; [38] and wherever the children of men dwell, or the beasts of the field and the birds of the heaven, He has given them into your hand, and has made you ruler over them all—you are this head of gold. [39] But after you shall arise another kingdom inferior to yours; then another, a third kingdom of bronze, which shall rule over all the earth. [40] And the fourth kingdom shall be as strong as iron, inasmuch as iron breaks in pieces and shatters everything; and like iron that crushes, that kingdom will break in pieces and crush all the others. 41 Whereas you saw the feet and toes, partly of potter's clay and partly of iron, the kingdom shall be divided; yet the strength of the iron shall be in it, just as you saw the iron mixed with ceramic clay. [42] And as the toes of the feet were partly of iron and partly of clay, so the kingdom shall be partly strong and partly [c]fragile. [43] As you saw iron mixed with ceramic clay, they will mingle with the seed of men; but they will not adhere to one another, just as iron does not mix with clay. [44] And in the days of these kings the God of heaven will set up a kingdom which shall never be destroyed; and the kingdom shall not be left to other people; it shall [d]break in pieces and [e]consume all these kingdoms, and it shall stand forever. [45] Inasmuch as you saw that the stone was cut out of the mountain without hands, and that it broke in pieces the iron, the bronze, the clay, the silver, and the gold—the great God has made known to the king what will come to pass after this. The dream is certain, and its interpretation is sure."

1 CORINTHIANS 6: 19-20

"[19] What? know ye not that your body is the temple of the Holy Ghost which is in you, which ye have of God, and ye are not your own? [20] For ye are bought with a price: therefore glorify God in your body, and in your spirit, which are God's."

76. See the Vaccines Adverse Event Reasoning System - *www.OpenVAERS.com/COVID-Data*

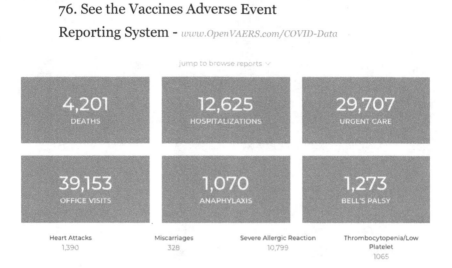

◊ NOTE: Less than 1% of vaccine injuries are ever entered into the vaccine adverse event reporting system.

Listen to What Is In the COVID-19 Vaccines Today On Rumble.com:

77.URGENT!!! Alarming Statistics of COVID-19 Vaccine Recipients (Bell's Palsy, Deaths, etc.)

https://rumble.com/vh3njv-urgent-alarming-statistics-of-covid-19-vaccine-recipients-bells-palsy-death.html

78.Doctor Christiane Northrup | What's Really in the COVID-19 Vaccinations?

https://rumble.com/vgzfxn-doctor-christiane-northrup-what-is-really-in-the-covid-vaccinations.html

79.What's In the COVID-19 Vaccines & How to Fight Back | Dr. Northrup & Attorney Leigh Dundas

https://rumble.com/vguyk5-whats-in-the-covid-19-vaccines-and-how-to-fight-back-dr.-northrup-and-attor.html

80.Dr. Carrie Madej | What Is In the COVID-19 Vaccines?

https://rumble.com/vggd8h-dr.-carrie-madej-what-is-in-the-covid-19-vaccines.html

CHAPTER 12

DID YOU KNOW THAT JEFFREY EPSTEIN HOPED TO CREATE HIS OWN RACE OF PEOPLE?

PRO TIP: It Is Generally Frowned Upon to Attempt to Create Your Own Race Of People

1.Jeffrey Epstein Hoped to Seed Human Race With His DNA

> **Jeffrey Epstein Hoped to Seed Human Race With His DNA**
> By James B. Stewart, Matthew Goldstein and Jessica Silver-Greenberg

https://www.nytimes.com/2019/07/31/business/jeffrey-epstein-eugenics.html

2.Epstein Reportedly Hoped to Develop Super-Race of Humans with His DNA

> Epstein reportedly hoped to develop super-race of humans with his DNA
>
> Registered sex offender hoped to seed human race with his DNA by impregnating 20 women at a time, New York Times reports

https://www.theguardian.com/us-news/2019/aug/01/jeffrey-epstein-seed-human-race-report

3.Jeffrey Epstein Reportedly Wanted to 'Seed the Human Race with his DNA' as Part of His Fascination with Transhumanism. Here's What That Means.

> **Jeffrey Epstein reportedly wanted to 'seed the human race with his DNA' as part of his fascination with transhumanism. Here's what that means.**

https://www.businessinsider.com/jeffrey-epstein-transhumanist-what-that-means-2019-7

4.Jeffrey Epstein 'Wanted to Seed Human Race with His DNA' by Impregnating Up to 20 Women At a Time, Report Says

> # Jeffrey Epstein 'wanted to seed human race with his DNA' by impregnating up to 20 women at a time, report says

https://www.independent.co.uk/news/world/americas/jeffrey-epstein-seed-human-race-dna-baby-ranch-new-mexico-eugenics-a9030411.html

MATTHEW CHAPTER 24:

"[1] And Jesus went out, and departed from the temple: and his disciples came to him for to shew him the buildings of the temple. [2] And Jesus said unto them, See ye not all these things? verily I say unto you, There shall not be left here one stone upon another, that shall not be thrown down. [3] And as he sat upon the mount of Olives, the disciples came unto him privately, saying, Tell us, when shall these things be? and what shall be the sign of thy coming, and of the end of the world? [4] And Jesus answered and said unto them, Take heed that no man deceive you. [5] For many shall come in my name, saying, I am Christ; and shall deceive many. [6] And ye shall hear of wars and rumours of wars: see that ye be not troubled: for all these things must come to pass, but the end is not yet. [7] For nation shall rise against nation, and kingdom against kingdom: and there shall be famines, and pestilences, and earthquakes, in divers places. [8] All these are the beginning of sorrows. [9] Then shall they deliver you up to be afflicted, and shall kill you: and ye shall be hated of all nations for my name's sake. [10] And then shall many be offended, and shall betray one another, and shall hate one another. [11] And many false prophets shall rise, and shall deceive many. [12] And because iniquity shall abound, the love of many shall wax cold. [13] But he that shall endure unto the end, the same shall be saved. [14] And this gospel of the kingdom shall be preached in all the world for a witness unto all nations; and then shall the end come. [15] When ye therefore shall see the abomination of desolation, spoken of by Daniel the prophet, stand in the holy place, (whoso readeth, let him understand:) [16] Then let them which be in Judaea flee into the mountains: [17] Let him which is on the housetop not come down to take any thing out of his house: [18] Neither let him which is in the field return back to take his clothes. [19] And woe unto them that are with child, and to them that give suck in those days! [20] But pray ye that your flight be not in the winter, neither on the sabbath day: [21] For then shall be great tribulation, such as was not since the beginning of the world to this time, no, nor ever shall be. [22] And except those days should be shortened, there should no flesh be saved: but for the elect's sake those days shall be shortened. [23] Then if any man shall say unto you, Lo, here is Christ, or there; believe it not. [24] For there shall arise false Christs, and false prophets, and shall shew great signs and wonders; insomuch that, if it were possible, they shall deceive the very elect. [25] Behold, I have told you before. [26] Wherefore if they shall say unto you, Behold, he is in the desert; go not forth: behold, he is in the secret chambers; believe it not. [27] For as the lightning cometh out of the east, and shineth even unto the west; so shall also the coming of the Son of man be. [28] For wheresoever the carcase is, there will the eagles be gathered together. [29] Immediately after the tribulation of those days shall the sun be darkened, and the moon shall not give her light, and the stars shall fall from heaven, and the powers of the heavens shall be shaken: [30] And then shall appear the sign of the Son of man in heaven: and then shall all the tribes of the earth mourn, and they shall see the Son of man coming in the clouds of heaven with power and great glory. [31] And he shall send his angels with a great sound of a trumpet, and they shall gather together his elect from the four winds, from one end of heaven to the other. [32] Now learn a parable of the fig tree; When his branch is yet tender, and putteth forth leaves, ye know that summer is nigh: [33] So likewise ye, when ye shall see all these things, know that it is near, even at the doors. [34] Verily I say unto you, This generation shall not pass, till all these things be fulfilled. [35] Heaven and earth shall pass away, but my words shall not pass away. [36] But of that day and hour knoweth no man, no, not the angels of heaven, but my Father only. [37] But as the days of Noah were, so shall also the coming of the Son of man be. [38] For as in the days that were before the flood they were eating and drinking, marrying and giving in marriage, until the day that Noe entered into the ark, [39] And knew not until the flood came, and took them all away; so shall also the coming of the Son of man be. [40] Then shall two be in the field; the one shall be taken, and the other left. [41] Two women shall be grinding at the mill; the one shall be taken, and the other left. [42] Watch therefore: for ye know not what hour your Lord doth come. [43] But know this, that if the goodman of the house had known in what watch the thief would come, he would have watched, and would not have suffered his house to be broken up. [44] Therefore be ye also ready: for in such an hour as ye think not the Son of man cometh. [45] Who then is a faithful and wise servant, whom his lord hath made ruler over his household, to give them meat in due season? [46] Blessed is that servant, whom his lord when he cometh shall find so doing. [47] Verily I say unto you, That he shall make him ruler over all his goods. [48] But and if that evil servant shall say in his heart, My lord delayeth his coming; [49] And shall begin to smite his fellowservants, and to eat and drink with the drunken; [50] The lord of that servant shall come in a day when he looketh not for him, and in an hour that he is not aware of, [51] And shall cut him asunder, and appoint him his portion with the hypocrites: there shall be weeping and gnashing of teeth."

CHAPTER 13

DID YOU KNOW THAT THE COVID-19 PANDEMIC WAS METHODICALLY AND NEFARIOUSLY PLANNED OUT BEGINNING OVER 10 YEARS AGO?

1. The Rockefeller Plan is Being Executed:

https://www.dropbox.com/s/ njzljlhebyjnqbz/Rockefeller%20 Foundation%20%281%29.pdf?dl=0

Scenarios for the Future of Technology and International Development

2. America is Being Destroyed From Within By Globalist Agents of the Great Reset

America Being Destroyed From Within By Globalist Agents of the Great Reset

https://79days.news/watch?id=6012f774ae174112e26ae4ac

3. The Truth About the COVID-19 Pandemic – The Real News

https://www.dropbox.com/s/ew6hfnoskmsxtaq/ The%20Truth%20About%20the%20 COVID-19%20Pandemic.pdf?dl=0

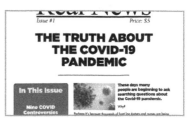

Issue #1   Price: $5

THE TRUTH ABOUT THE COVID-19 PANDEMIC

In This Issue

These days many people are beginning to ask searching questions about the Covid-19 pandemic.

Why?

Nine COVID Controversies

4.Investigative Journalist Harry Vox reads The Rockefeller Plan:

https://www.bitchute.com/video/lQ8trYUxwHJg/

HARRY VOX | HE WARNED ABOUT LOCKDOWNS AND QUARANTINE IN 2014

WATCH

5.From a Conspiracy Theory to Official Government Policy in 3 Months | Forced Quarantines in Designated Government Facilities and Mandatory COVID-19 Testing Becomes a Reality

https://www.bitchute.com/video/DDbJb49oz6pt/

FROM A CONSPIRACY THEORY TO OFFICIAL GOVERNMENT POLICY IN 3 MONTHS

WATCH

6.Read the Richard A. Rothschild Patent – A method is provided for acquiring and transmitting bio-metric data

https://patentimages.storage.googleapis.com/61/a3/od/3d91325d909386/US20200279585A1.pdf

7.Launching the Decade of Vaccines

> ## Global Health Leaders Launch Decade of Vaccines Collaboration | Bill & Melinda Gates Foundation

https://www.gatesfoundation.org/Media-Center/Press-Releases/2010/12/Global-Health-Leaders-Launch-Decade-of-Vaccines-Collaboration

8.Al Gore Calls for "Global Reset" of Capitalism

> OPINION | COMMENTARY
> ## *Capitalism After the Coronavirus*
> The pandemic provides an opportunity to build a resilient, healthy, fair and zero-carbon econor

https://www.wsj.com/articles/capitalism-after-the-coronavirus-11593470102

9.Al Gore and U.N. Secretary General Call
for Global Reset of Capitalism

Al Gore, UN Secretary-General, others now demanding 'Great Reset' of global capitalism

These are truly dangerous times for those who support individual liberty and free markets

https://www.foxbusiness.com/markets/al-gore-un-secretary-general-great-reset-global-capitalism

10.Event 201

https://www.centerforhealthsecurity.org/event201/

11.Event 201 Explained in Detail

https://www.youtube.com/watch?v=AoLw-Q8X174&feature=youtu.be&t=493

12.Mayors Challenge

Mayors Challenge

Inspiring bold, replicable innovations developed by cities

https://www.bloomberg.org/program/government-innovation/mayors-challenge/

13.Implementing a National COVID-19 Testing Action Plan

National Covid-19 Testing Action Plan Pragmatic steps to reopen our workplaces and our communities

https://www.rockefellerfoundation.org/wp-content/uploads/2020/04/TheRockefellerFoundation_WhitePaper_Covid19_4_22_2020.pdf

14.Implementing a Digital Immunity Certificate

https://www.youtube.com/watch?time_continue=23&v=LsNfyzuDvQo&feature=emb_title

15.Implementing the COVI-Pass
https://covipass.com/

ONE PLATFORM. SIX COMPREHENSIVE SOLUTIONS.

16.Implementing the "Trust Stamp" Vaccine Record and Payment System
https://citizentruth.org/africa-to-become-testing-ground-for-trust-stamp-vaccine-record-and-payment-system/

Africa to Become Testing Ground for "Trust Stamp" Vaccine Record and Payment System

17.Efficiently delivering vaccines to millions of children, tracking identity and immunisation records in a digitised manner and incentivising the delivery of vaccines

PROCEEDS TO GAVI FROM DONOR CONTRIBUTIONS & PLEDGES (2016-2020) AS OF 30 SEPTEMBER 2020

https://www.gavi.org/investing-gavi/funding/donor-profiles/mastercard

PSALM 54

"[1] Save me, O God, by thy name, and judge me by thy strength. [2] Hear my prayer, O God; give ear to the words of my mouth. [3] For strangers are risen up against me, and oppressors seek after my soul: they have not set God before them. Selah. [4] Behold, God is mine helper: the Lord is with them that uphold my soul. [5] He shall reward evil unto mine enemies: cut them off in thy truth. [6] I will freely sacrifice unto thee: I will praise thy name, O Lord; for it is good. [7] For he hath delivered me out of all trouble: and mine eye hath seen his desire upon mine enemies."

CHAPTER 14

DID YOU KNOW THAT THE ORGANIZATION THAT HIJACKED THE PHRASE AND THE SENTIMENT BEHIND THE PHRASE "BLACK LIVES MATTER" IS LED BY TRAINED MARXISTS WHO OPENLY PRAYS TO THE DEMON SPIRIT OF "IFA"?

1."Black Lives Matter the Sentiment I Can Get Behind. Black Lives Matter the Organization I Cannot Get Behind." – Colion Noir – *https://www.youtube.com/watch?v=rc-37d8yrO4*

2."We are trained Marxists." – Black Lives Matter Founding Member Patrisse Cullors *https://www.bitchute.com/ video/wM7Lziw65yBP/*

3.Susan Rosenberg, a Member of the Board of Directors for the Left-Wing Thousand Currents Group, Which Handles the Intake of Donations Made to Black Lives Matter, is a Convicted Terrorist. She was convicted for the

1983 bombing of the United States Capitol Building, the
U.S. Naval War College, and the New York Patrolmen's
Benevolent
Association. She was released from prison after serving
16 years of her 58-year prison sentence when Bill Clinton
commuted her sentence on his last day in office.

Black Lives Matter fundraising handled by group with convicted terrorist on its board

by Jerry Dunleavy, Justice Department Reporter | ✉ | June 25, 2020 08:25 PM

---

https://www.washingtonexaminer.com/news/black-lives-matter-fundraising-handled-by-group-with-convicted-terrorist-on-its-board

4. "Black Lives Matter Is a
Marxist Organization." –
Professor Carol M. Swain,
Ph.D.

https://www.youtube.
com/watch?v=rpLItQnrgec&feature=share&fbclid=IwAR1LgoRLyFT-
JwTFjvlKREwQeZx3xlozzDuvkqSDhnRcAe5zoKA9FQMu4Rg8

5. Charles Wade, a Black Lives Matter co-founder Was
Arrested Charged with Human Trafficking and Prostitution.

Black Lives Matter leader Charles Wade charged with sex trafficking 📄

---

https://www.washingtontimes.com/news/2016/may/19/
charles-wade-black-lives-matter-leader-charged-wit/

6. "Here is the employee chart for ActBlue Charities— the
company that receives every dollar raised via the Black
Lives Matter website. The entire company is composed of
white left-wing political activists who you can research.
They also run the ACTBLUE super PAC." – Candace Owens

Candace Owens ✓ @RealCandaceO · Jun 10, 2020
Here is the employee chart for ActBlue Charities— the company that
receives every dollar raised via the Black Lives Matter website.

https://twitter.com/RealCandaceO/status/1270897291038244864?s=20

7.FACTS: Watch An Interview with George Soros (the Man Funding the Riots) Explain How He Did Not Feel Bad

Working Directly with the NAZI's to Steal Property from Jewish People: WATCH 6:38-9:03

https://youtu.be/AiqHiQYuoOs?t=408

8.SOROS Donates $33 Million to Black Lives Matter Movement

https://www.washingtontimes.com/news/2016/aug/16/black-lives-matter-cashes-100-million-liberal-foun/

Black Lives Matter cashes in with $100 million from liberal foundations

9.AUGUST 1st 2016 – Released Aug. 1, the Black Lives Matter Movement also calls for defunding police

PLATFORM

departments, race-based reparations, breaking, voting rights for illegal immigrants, fossil-fuel divestment, an end to private education and charter schools, a "universal basic income," and free college for blacks. (NOW DELETED)

https://web.archive.org/web/20200223061853/https://policy.m4bl.org/platform/

10.Candace Owens shares the FACTS with great conviction:

https://youtu.be/-Bo2c3ZYsCQ?t=57

11.The Conservative Twins stand up for the police:

https://www.youtube.com/watch?v=gJffxP4lBzQ

12. Why Did George Soros Endorse Bill De Blasio for Mayor of New York City?

https://www.nytimes.com/2013/08/07/ nyregion/soros-to-endorse-de-blasio- for-mayor.html?auth=login-google

TRAILSIDE

Soros Endorses de Blasio for Mayor

f ⊙ ♥ ✉ ↗

By Michael M. Grynbaum

Aug. 6, 2013

In a move that could excite left-leaning New Yorkers — but turn away some more centrist ones — the billionaire financier and liberal icon George Soros endorsed Bill de Blasio, the public advocate, on Tuesday as the next mayor of New York.

13. Why Is George Soros Connected to Ocasio-Cortez?

US NEWS

Details of Ocasio-Cortez's Ties To George Soros Revealed

By The Daily Caller News Foundation
Published August 19, 2018 at 3:56pm

DAILY CALL
NEWS FOUNDAT

https://thefederalistpapers.org/us/details-ocasio-cortezs-ties-george-soros

14. Why Did Chicago Launch a Soros-Backed Coronavirus Fund for Illegals?

https://www.newswars.com/chicago-launches- soros-backed-coronavirus-fund-for-illegals/

Chicago Launches Soros-Backed Coronavirus Fund For Illegals

Mayor Lori Lightfoot announces $5 million cash program

15. Why is Black Lives Matter Supporting Washington's Disgraced Governor Inslee for Re-Election?

Chip In to Support Jay Inslee's Reelection	1) Amount	2) Details	3) Payment
Early to bed, early to rise, work like hell and organize.	Your contribution will benefit Jay Inslee.		

https://secure.actblue.com/donate/jay-inslee-4

16. Why Did George Soros Make Major Donations to Get California's Governor Gavin Newsom Elected?

f ✆ ✉

Track the millions flowing into California's race for governor

By RYAN MENEZES AND MALOY MOORE

UPDATED NOV. 5, 2018

Here's where things stand as the Nov. 6 election approaches

https://www.latimes.com/projects/la-pol-ca-california-governor-2018-money/

17. Black Lives Matter Activists Corner Woman At Restaurant, Demand She Raise Fist. She Refuses. *https://www.dailywire.com/news/watch-black-lives-matter-activists-corner-woman-at-restaurant-demand-she-raise-fist-she-refuses?utm_source=facebook&utm_medium=social&utm_campaign=benshapiro&fbclid=IwAR273yAuK-M1lWNaHzBYUiVqndHnGVhRwVqKkmsEN5BLcSc62QP1iQsqrNt8*

> NEWS AND COMMENTARY
>
> **WATCH: Black Lives Matter Activists Corner Woman At Restaurant, Demand She Raise Fist. She Refuses.**
>
> By Ryan Saavedra
>
> Aug 25, 2020 DailyWire.com

18. Electing Marxist / Communists to Implement the Written Plan

   ◇ a. Did You Know New York City's Bill de Blasio Changed His Name So That You Wouldn't Remember That He Was Once an Outspoken Marxist?

   ◇ b. The Mayor of New York City Bill de Blasio's birth name was Warren Wilhelm, Jr.

   ◇ c. New York Mayor Bill de Blasio was previously named "Warren Wilhelm Jr." and once supported the socialist government of the Sandinistas in Nicaragua.

   > **Did NYC Mayor Bill de Blasio Once Support the Sandinista Govt. in Nicaragua?**
   >
   > In May 2019, social media posts targeted the would-be 2020 Democratic presidential nominee for his past political positions, as well as his decision to change his name.

   https://www.snopes.com/fact-check/deblasio-nicaragua-warren-wilhelm/

   ◇ d. The man who could become the city's 109th mayor was born Warren Wilhelm Jr. on May 8, 1961, in Manhattan, his birth certificate shows.

   > **Mayoral hopeful Bill de Blasio has had three different legal names, court records show**

   https://www.nydailynews.com/news/election/de-blasio-names-de-blasio-article-1.1463591

19.Black Lives Matter Co-
Founder Teams Up with Chinese
Advocacy Group

https://nypost.com/2020/09/17/
blm-co-founder-teams-up-with-
chinese-advocacy-group/

23.Did You See the Magic U-Haul
Truck Filled With Riot Gear?
Do You Know Who Funded It?

⋄   a.See the truck filled with
    riot supplies for pro-
    testers —*https://www.youtube.*
    com/watch?v=MQSJhHOSAw4

⋄   b.Holly Zoller, who works at
    The Bail Project,
    rented the truck
    https://bailproject.org/team/holly-zoller/

⋄   c.The Bail Project has many
    donors
    https://bailproject.org/wp-con-
    tent/uploads/2021/02/TBP_An-
    nual_Report_2019.pdf

⋄   d.These people donated $5,000,000+ to the proj-
    ect —Micheal Novagrazt
    — Board member of The
    Bail Project *https://www.*
    google.com/search?q=what+does+-
    micheal+novagrazt+do&rlz=1C-
    1CHBF_enUS849US849&oq=what+-
    does+micheal+novagrazt+do&aqs=-
    chrome..69i57.6543j0j1&sourceid=chrome&ie=UTF-8

◊   e.The Blue Meridian Group

https://www.bluemeridian.org/our-partners/

CHAPTER 15

WHY ARE THE SCIENTIST NOT REPORTING THE TRUTH ABOUT COVID-19?

Should We Trust The Scientist?

A. It is alleged that, unbeknownst to Harvard University, beginning in 2011, Dr. Charles Lieber became a "Strategic Scientist" at Wuhan University of Technology (WUT) in China. He later became contractual participant in China's Thousand Talents Plan from at least 2012 through 2015.

JUSTICE NEWS		RELATED LINKS
	Department of Justice	Speeches and Press Releases
	Office of Public Affairs	Videos
		Photos
FOR IMMEDIATE RELEASE	Tuesday, June 9, 2020	Blogs
		Podcasts
Harvard University Professor Indicted on False Statement Charges		
The former Chair of Harvard University's Chemistry and Chemical Biology Department was indicted today on charges of making false statements to federal authorities regarding his participation in China's Thousand Talents Program.		

https://www.justice.gov/opa/pr/harvard-university-professor-indicted-false-statement-charges

B. Fifty-four scientists have lost their jobs as a result of NIH probe into foreign ties

> ### Fifty-four scientists have lost their jobs as a result of NIH probe into foreign ties
>
> By **Jeffrey Mervis** | Jun. 12, 2020 , 6:00 PM

https://www.sciencemag.org/news/2020/06/fifty-four-scientists-have-lost-their-jobs-result-nih-probe-foreign-ties

C. 500 U.S. Scientists Feared Compromised by China!!!!

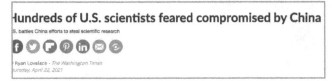

https://m.washingtontimes.com/news/2021/apr/22/us-scientists-feared-compromised-china/

D. Harvard University Professor and Two Chinese Nationals Charged in Three Separate China Related Cases

> ### Harvard University Professor and Two Chinese Nationals Charged in Three Separate China Related Cases
>
> The Department of Justice announced today that the Chair of Harvard University's Chemistry and Chemical Biology Department and two Chinese nationals have been charged in connection with aiding the People's Republic of China.

https://www.justice.gov/opa/pr/harvard-university-professor-and-two-chinese-nationals-charged-three-separate-china-related

E. Acclaimed Harvard Scientist Is Arrested, Accused Of Lying About Ties To China

LAW

Acclaimed Harvard Scientist Is Arrested, Accused Of Lying About Ties To China

January 28, 2020 · 2:31 PM ET

BILL CHAPPELL

https://www.npr.org/2020/01/28/800442646/acclaimed-harvard-scientist-is-arrested-accused-of-lying-about-ties-to-china

DID YOU KNOW THAT THE ORGANIZATION THAT HIJACKED THE PHRASE AND THE SENTIMINENT BEHIND THE PHRASE "BLACK LIVES MATTER" IS FUNDED BY A WHITE MAN WHO OPENLY UNAPOLOGETICALLY ADMITTED TO BEING A NAZI ON 60 MINUTES?

1.Follow the Money and You Will Find George Soros and His Plan to Destroy America

https://rumble.com/vdnxiz-special-billionaire-radical-george-soros-his-plan-to-destroy-america.html

2.George Soros 1998 60 Minutes Interview by 60 Minutes

https://www.bitchute.com/video/ztwkuXgXmLot/

2 THESSALONIANS 8-12

"8 And then shall that Wicked be revealed, whom the Lord shall consume with the spirit of his mouth, and shall destroy with the brightness of his coming: 9 Even him, whose coming is after the working of Satan with all power and signs and lying wonders, 10 And with all deceivableness of unrighteousness in them that perish; because they received not the love of the truth, that they might be saved. [11] And for this cause God shall send them strong delusion, that they should believe a lie: [12] That they all might be damned who believed not the truth, but had pleasure in unrighteousness."

CHAPTER 17

DID YOU KNOW THAT THE DOMINION VOTING MACHINE COMPANY SHARED OFFICE SPACE WITH GEORGE SOROS AT 221 SPADINA AVENUE IN TORONTO, ONTARIO?

1.Prolific Entrepreneur Jovan Pulitzer Explains How Technology Was Used to Commit Election Fraud

https://www.bitchute.com/video/eoMQWtObVm5r/

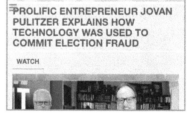

2.January 8th 2021 – Lance Wallnau: Rudy Giuliani – Drops Bombshell! We Got Them! JUST IN

https://www.bitchute.com/video/EqUQzdO8NayG/

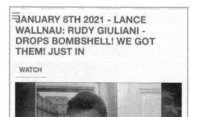

3.Read Sidney Powell's 270 Page Report On 2020 Foreign Election Interference, Mass Voter Fraud

https://wpcdn.zenger.news/wp-content/uploads/2020/12/24190822/2020-12-23-Sidney-Powell-Team-Binder-ZENGER-NEWS.pdf

4.WATCH – Election Machines Were Connected to the Internet, Georgia Hearing Reveals LIVE, Real-time HACKING of Dominion Voting Systems. Expert Witness and Prolific Inventor / Entrepreneur | Jovan Hutton Pulitzer

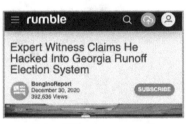

https://rumble.com/vcalln-expert-witness-claims-he-hacked-into-georgia-runoff-election-system.html

5.BREAKING – GAME OVER: Dominion voting Machines LIVE HACKED During Georgia Senate Hearing!!!

https://www.naturalnews.com/2020-12-30-game-over-dominion-voting-machines-live-hacked-georgia-election.html

6.2020 Election Investigative Documentary: Who's Stealing America?

Did NYC Mayor Bill de Blasio Once Support the Sandinista Govt. in Nicaragua?

In May 2019, social media posts targeted the would-be 2020 Democratic presidential nominee for his past political positions, as well as his decision to change his name.

https://www.theepochtimes.com/2020-election-investigation-who-is-stealing-america_3617562.html?utm_medium=email&utm_source=promotion&utm_campaign=EET1216&utm_term=1for4M-ElectionDocumentary&utm_content=video

7.Election Night Errors Explained

https://rumble.com/vbu6xh-election-night-errors-how-did-that-happen.html

JOHN 8:44

"Ye are of your father the devil, and the lusts of your father ye will do. He was a murderer from the beginning, and abode not in the truth, because there is no truth in him. When he speaketh a lie, he speaketh of his own: for he is a liar, and the father of it."

CHAPTER 18

DID YOU KNOW THAT THE HEAD OF STRATEGY AND SECURITY FOR THE DOMINION VOTING MACHINE COMPANY (ERIC COOMER) PROUDLY BRAGGED THAT HE "MADE SURE" TRUMP WOULDN'T WIN, REPORT SAYS?

1.Dominion Engineer Told Antifa He'd "Made Sure" Trump Wouldn't Win, Report Says

https://newsthud.com/dominion-engineer-told-antifa-hed-made-sure-trump-wouldnt-win-report-says/

NEWS ← US NEWS

Dominion Engineer Told Antifa He'd "Made Sure" Trump Wouldn't Win, Report Says

written by Neon Nettle

November 15, 2020

Vice President of U.S. Engineering Eric Coomer shared anti-Trump posts online

2017 - The Director of Product Strategy and Security for Dominion Voting Systems Eric Coomer Explains How to Alter Votes Using the DOMINION Voting System

https://rumble.com/vbd3s5-2017-dr.-eric-coomer-explains-how-to-alter-votes-in-the-dominion-voting-sys.html

The Director of Product Strategy and Security for Dominion Voting Systems Joe Oltmann tweeted a few screenshots of a Facebook user posting Antifa manifestos and songs about killing police. –

https://www.theamericanconservative.com/articles/the-extremist-at-dominion-voting-systems/

Read Sidney Powell's 270 Page Report Explaining How Election Fraud and Foriegn Interference in the 2020 Elections Was Carried Out

https://wpcdn.zenger.news/wp-content/uploads/2020/12/24190822/2020-12-23-Sidney-Powell-Team-Binder-ZENGER-NEWS.pdf

Joe Oltmann | Exposing the Treasonous Eric Coomer the ANTIFA Member and the Director of Strategy and Security at DOMINION Voting Systems

Joe Oltmann | Exposing the Treasonous Eric Coomer the ANTIFA Member and the Director of Strategy and Security at DOMINION Voting Systems

thrivetimeshow · Published December 21, 2020 · 4,804 Views

SUBSCRIBE   SHARE

https://rumble.com/vc2jp7-joe-oltmann-exposing-treasonous-eric-coomer-with-the-antifa.html

Watch Absolute Proof | Discover The 100% Irrefutable Proof of the 2020 Election Fraud

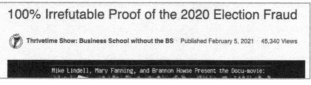

100% Irrefutable Proof of the 2020 Election Fraud

Thrivetime Show: Business School without the BS · Published February 5, 2021 · 45,340 Views

Mike Lindell, Mary Fanning, and Brannon Howse Present the Docu-movie:

https://rumble.com/vdlgg1-100-irrefutable-proof-of-the-2020-election-fraud.html

DID YOU KNOW THAT THE FOUNDER OF THE QR CODE JOVAN HUTTON PULITZER DISCOVERED THAT THOUSANDS UPON THOUSANDS OF MAIL-IN BALLOTS WERE NEVER FOLDED AND THUS THEY WERE FRAUDULENT AND NEVER MAILED?

Watch Jovan Hutton-Pultizer explain how widespread systematic election fraud was orchestrated

Jovan Hutton Pulitzer I Election Fraud Explained In Simple Terms (Even Clay Can Understand)

Thrivetime Show: Business School without the BS · Published May 4, 2021 · 12,232 Views · SUBSCRIBE 149K · SHARE

https://rumble.com/vghfhp-jovan-hutton-pulitzer-election-fraud-explained-in-simple-terms-even-clay-ca.html

Watch - Joe Oltmann | Exposing the Treasonous Eric Coomer the ANTIFA Member and the Director of Strategy and Security at DOMINION Voting Systems

Joe Oltmann I Exposing the Treasonous Eric Coomer the ANTIFA Member and the Director of Strategy and Security at DOMINION Voting Systems

https://rumble.com/vc2jp7-joe-oltmann-exposing-treasonous-eric-coomer-with-the-antifa.html

Watch - "Trump Will Not Win" Says DOMINION Executive Eric Coomer

https://www.bitchute.com/ video/qOMHY63ntkCv/

Watch - DOMINION's Eric Coomer Admits Voting Machines Use Wireless Internet Connections

NEW VIDEO SHOWS DOMINION ERIC COOMER ADMITTING VOTING MACHINE USE WIRELESS INTERNET AND SUPPORT AL..

https://www.bitchute.com/video/ALom1IsQn5U/

Watch - Dominion Eric Coomer Taped Saying To ANTIFA " Don't Worry Trump Won't Win We Fixed That"

https://www.bitchute.com/video/ynn32H1wlItH/

Watch - 2017 - Eric Coomer Explains How to Alter Votes in the DOMINION Voting System

2017 DR. ERIC COOMER EXPLAINS HOW TO ALTER VOTES IN THE DOMINION VOTING SYSTEM

https://rumble.com/vbd3s5-2017-dr.-eric-coomer-explains- how-to-alter-votes-in-the-dominion-voting-sys.html

DID YOU KNOW THAT THE SOFTWARE USED IN THE 2020 ELECTIONS WAS CREATED BY A COMPANY (SMARTMATIC) THAT WAS FOUNDED AND FUNDED BY COMMUNIST VENEZUELANS TO SWITCH THE VOTES NEEDED TO SUCCESSFULLY PUT THE COMMUNIST MADURO AND CHAVEZ FAMILIES INTO POWER?

1. The Venezuelan Communist Dictator Hugo Chavez Built SMARTMATIC – The CEO of OverStock.com (Patrick Byrne) Explains the Technical Details of How Votes Were Stole and Switched – Watch at 7:00 Minutes

   Tech Expert Patrick Byrne Explains How They Used "Stop and Drop" To Steal The

   https://americalatestnews.com/tech-expert-patrick-byrne-explains-how-they-used-stop-and-drop-to-steal-the-election/

2. Neffenger on Biden's "transition team" is on board of Smartmatic

   Trump attorney Sidney Powell says they are 'fixing to overturn the results of the election in several

   https://www.washingtonexaminer.com/news/trump-attorney-sidney-powell-says-they-are-fixing-to-overturn-the-results-of-the-election-in-several-states

3. STATISTICAL PROOF: "Smartmatic" Vote-Counting System Was Manipulated in PA and GA to Overturn Trump's Victory

> "DNA-LEVEL" STATISTICAL PROOF: "Smartmatic" Vote-Counting System Was Manipulated in PA and GA to Overturn Trump's Victory
>
> The charts below are derived from *The New York Times'* real-time election feeds (e.g., here). They show "DNA-level" evidence of vote fraud that was systematically used to overcome
>
> Tweet   👍 Like 27K

http://directorblue.blogspot.com/2020/11/dna-level-statistical-proof-smartmatic.html

4. BLAST FROM THE PAST: Smartmatic CEO Introduces Creepy Bill Gates at Global Citizen Conference in June 2015

> **BLAST FROM THE PAST: Smartmatic CEO Introduces Creepy Bill Gates at Global Citizen Conference in June 2015**

https://www.thegatewaypundit.com/2020/11/blast-past-smartmatic-ceo-introduces-creepy-bill-gates-global-citizen-conference-june-2015/

5. Whistleblowers Explain How the Venezuelan Communist Created SMARTMATIC Software Changes Election Results –

> # Whistleblower Alleges Software Manipulated Votes to Change

https://link.theepochtimes.com/mkt_app/whistleblowers-reveal-how-software-manipulates-votes-to-change-election-results_3581769.html

6. What Do Smartmatic and George Soros Have in Common? Lord Mark Malloch-Brown is a Board Member on Both Organizations

> ## Lord Mark Malloch-Brown
>
> Chairman

https://web.archive.org/web/20201107150930/https://www.smartmatic.com/us/about/leadership/detail/lord-mark-malloch-brown/
https://www.opensocietyfoundations.org/who-we-are/boards/global-board/member/mark-malloch-brown

7. The Smartmatic Story:
   From Venezuela With No Love –

Supreme Court to Consider Case Alleging Harvard Anti-Asian Bias in Admissions

https://www.theepochtimes.com/the-smartmatic-story-from-venezuela-with-no-love_3592443.html

8. Wikileaks: Soros-Linked Voting Machines Now Used in Most Battleground States Were Used to Rig the 2004 Venezuela Elections

Wikileaks: Soros-Linked Voting Machines Now Used in Most Battleground States Were Used to Rig the 2004 Venezuela Elections

https://www.thegatewaypundit.com/2020/11/wikileaks-soros-linked-voting-machines-now-used-battleground-states-used-rig-2004-venezuela-elections/

9. CIA, Gina Haspel and Hugo Chavez' SmartMatic Behind USA Steal –

Featured

CIA, Gina Haspel and Hugo Chavez' SmartMatic Behind USA Steal

by David Knight | RoundTableReport.com
November 17th 2020, 11:17 am

https://www.infowars.com/posts/cia-gina-haspel-and-hugo-chavez-smartmatic-behind-usa-steal/

10. The People Behind the SMARTMATIC software –

4 Things to Know About Voting Machine Company That's Causing Stir

Fred Lucas / @FredLucasWH / November 09, 2020

https://www.dailysignal.com/2020/11/09/4-things-to-know-about-voting machine-company-thats-causing-stir/

11. Smartmatic Denies Transfer of Technology to Dominion Voting Systems — Articles Scrubbed from Website — But Internet Archive Never Lies –

Smartmatic Denies Transfer of Technology to Dominion Voting Systems – Articles Scrubbed from

https://www.thegatewaypundit.com/2020/11/smartmatic-denies-transfer-technology-dominion-voting-systems-articles-scrubbed-website-internet-archive-never-lies/

12. The link Between Dominion, Sequoia, Smartmatic, and the CCP

> ## The link Between Dominion, Sequoia, Smartmatic, and the CCP

https://gnews.org/577635/

13. Lou Dobbs on CNN in 2006: Smartmatic based in Venezuela sold  to Dominion, top officials in Venezuela

https://www.3.com/watch?v=RvYSuJwXp9Q&feature=youtu.be

14. Roger Stone reveals that Microsoft designed a software  called "ElectionGuard" that is being used by DOMINION, Election Services, Heart Intercivic, Clean Ballot Election Systems and Hardware B-Pro and Smartmatic. 100% of the voting machines and voting systems in this country are using "ElectionGuard." –

https://www.youtube.com/watch?feature=youtu. be&v=YtjL6KFO5eU&app=desktop

CHAPTER 21

THE CALL TO ACTION

1.You and I must return our focus to God, to sharing the Gospel and to living as instructed us to do in His word (The Bible).

2.You and I must get involved in local, and national politics.

"Freedom is never more than one generation away from extinction. We didn't pass it to our children in the bloodstream. It must be fought for, protected, and handed on for them to do the same, or one day we will spend our sunset years telling our children and our children's children what it was once like in the United States where men were free."

- President Ronald Reagan
(The 40th President of the United States)

"¹⁰ Blessed are they which are persecuted for righteousness' sake: for theirs is the kingdom of heaven. ¹¹ Blessed are ye, when men shall revile you, and persecute you, and shall say all manner of evil against you falsely, for my sake."

- MATTHEW 5:10-11

3.You and I must look for ways to not financially support the Globalist organizations and people who seek to implement the "Great Reset".

¹³ Enter ye in at the strait gate: for wide is the gate, and broad is the way, that leadeth to destruction, and many there be which go in thereat:

¹⁴ Because strait is the gate, and narrow is the way, which leadeth unto life, and few there be that find it.

¹⁵ Beware of false prophets, which come to you in sheep's clothing, but inwardly they are ravening wolves.

¹⁶ Ye shall know them by their fruits. Do men gather grapes of thorns, or figs of thistles?

¹⁷ Even so every good tree bringeth forth good fruit; but a corrupt tree bringeth forth evil fruit.

¹⁸ A good tree cannot bring forth evil fruit, neither can a corrupt tree bring forth good fruit.

¹⁹ Every tree that bringeth not forth good fruit is hewn down, and cast into the fire.

²⁰ Wherefore by their fruits ye shall know them.

²¹ Not every one that saith unto me, Lord, Lord, shall enter into the kingdom of heaven; but he that doeth the will of my Father which is in heaven.

²² Many will say to me in that day, Lord, Lord, have we not prophesied in thy name? and in thy name have we cast out devils? and in thy name done many wonderful works?

²³ And then will I profess unto them, I never knew you: depart from me, ye that work iniquity.

²⁴ Therefore whosoever heareth these sayings of mine, and doeth them, I will liken him unto a wise man, which built his house upon a rock:

²⁵ And the rain descended, and the floods came, and the winds blew, and beat upon that house; and it fell not: for it was founded upon a rock.

²⁶ And every one that heareth these sayings of mine, and doeth them not, shall be likened unto a foolish man, which built his house upon the sand:

²⁷ And the rain descended, and the floods came, and the winds blew, and beat upon that house; and it fell: and great was the fall of it.

²⁸ And it came to pass, when Jesus had ended these sayings, the people were astonished at his doctrine:

²⁹ For he taught them as one having authority, and not as the scribes.

CHAPTER 22

DID YOU KNOW THAT GEORGE SOROS IS PAYING PASTORS TO ENDORSE THE GLOBALIST AGENDA?

1. Christian Groups Take Money from Atheist Billionaire George Soros

   Tech Expert Patrick Byrne Explains How They Used "Stop and Drop" To Steal The Election

   © November 24, 2020   admin   NEWS   Comments Off

   Patrick Byrne is the founder of Overstock.com and by all accounts probably a genius in the realms of data

   https://youtu.be/O5DyqOezBaw

2. Dr. Fauci Meets with T.D. Jakes & Other Religious

   NEWS › PUBLIC HEALTH

   'We're all in this together': Fauci speaks on panel with T.D. Jakes about COVID-19 vaccines

   Fauci, the nation's top infectious disease official and adviser to President Biden, and the panel sought to quell distrust about the coronavirus vaccines, especially among Black Americans.

   Leaders

   https://www.dallasnews.com/news/public-health/2021/01/25/were-all-in-this-together-facui-speaks-on-panel-with-td-jakes-about-covid-19-vaccines/

3. Soros Co-opting Churches to Push New World Order

Soros Co-opting Churches to Push New World Order

by Alex Newman   April 5, 2016

https://thenewamerican.com/soros-co-opting-churches-to-push-new-world-order/

4. George Soros and his 'rented evangelicals' outed by Christian leaders -

George Soros and his 'rented evangelicals' outed by Christian leaders

https://www.washingtontimes.com/news/2018/oct/22/george-soros-and-his-rented-evangelicals-outed-chr/

5. Christian "Leaders" Who Endorsed Joe Biden are Leftists Funded by George Soros

Christian "Leaders" Who Endorsed Joe Biden are Leftists Funded by George Soros

https://www.lifenews.com/2020/10/09/christian-leaders-who-endorsed-joe-biden-are-leftists-funded-by-george-soros/

6. YEAR IN REVIEW: How George Soros 'Rents' Evangelicals to Confuse Voters

YEAR IN REVIEW: How George Soros 'Rents' Evangelicals to Confuse Voters

https://www.charismanews.com/us/73708-how-george-soros-rents-evangelicals-to-confuse-voters

7. Is Billionaire Atheist George Soros Secretly Paying for Evangelicals' Pro-Immigration Reform Efforts

Is Billionaire Atheist George Soros Secretly Paying for Evangelicals' Pro-Immigration Reform Efforts?

https://www.theblaze.com/news/2013/06/24/is-george-soros-secretly-funding-evangelicals-pro-immigration-reform-efforts

CHAPTER 23

SHOULD YOU TRUST A MAINSTREAM MEDIA CONTROLLED BY JUST 6 CORPORATIONS?

1. NOTABLE QUOTABLE - "If you tell a lie big enough and keep repeating it, people will eventually come to believe it." - Joseph Goebbels (Nazi propaganda chief)

2. Top U.S. Media Outlets "Compromised" by Communist China - *https://thenewamerican.com/top-u-s-media-outlets-compromised-by-communist-china/*

3. These 6 Corporations Control 90% of the Media Outlets in America. Discover the Illusion of Choice and Objectivity
   *https://techstartups.
   com/2020/09/18/6-corporations-
   control-90-media-america-
   illusion-choice-objectivity-2020/*

4. FACEBOOK CONTENT MODERATOR: 'IF SOMEONE'S WEARING MAGA HAT, I'M GOING TO DELETE THEM FOR TERRORISM'
   https://www.bitchute.com/

5. Hawley blasts big tech for 'censoring' Christian worship leader

Hawley blasts big tech for 'censoring' Christian worship leader

   *https://www.foxnews.com/politics/hawley-blasts-
   big-tech-censoring-christian-worship-leader*

6. Bethel Music's Sean Feucht calls out Instagram, Twitter for censoring Bible verses, worship videos *https://
   www.christianpost.com/news/
   bethel-musics-sean-feucht-calls-out-
   instagram-twitter-for-censoring-
   bible-verses-worship-videos.html*

Bethel Music's Sean Feucht calls out Instagram, Twitter for censoring Bible verses, worship videos

By Anugrah Kumar, Christian Post Contributor

7. "If you don't have enough evidence to see this charade, then you need to get your head out of the sand." – Pastor Rob McCoy (Calvary Chapel) –

https://youtu.be/oTfooenZU6g?t=1223

CHAPTER 24

WHAT'S THEIR MOTIVE? THEY ARE THE DEVIL'S ADVOCATE

JOHN 10:10

King James Version10 The thief cometh not, but for to steal, and to kill, and to destroy: I am come that they might have life, and that they might have it more abundantly.

1. Why does the CDC call for Nazi style quarantine/ concentration camps to stop the spread of nearly 100% treatable virus? (Covid-19)

Shielding Approach to Prevent COVID-19 Infections in Humanitarian Settings

Updated July 26, 2020   Print

https://www.cdc.gov/coronavirus/2019-ncov/global-covid-19/shielding-approach-humanitarian.html

2. Why did Microsoft file for the CRYPTOCURRENCY SYSTEM USING BODY ACTIVITY DATA with a publication number of W02020060606

1. W02020060606 - CRYPTOCURRENCY SYSTEM USING BODY ACTIVITY DATA

PCT Biblio. Data Description Claims Drawings ISR/WOSA/AI7I2[a] Patent Family Notices Documents

https://patentscope.wipo.int/search/en/detail.jsf?docId=WO2020060606

REVELATION CHAPTER 13: 16

And he causeth all, both small and great, rich and poor, free and bond, to receive a mark in their right hand, or in their foreheads:

17 And that no man might buy or sell, save he that had the mark, or the name of the beast, or the number of his name.

18 Here is wisdom. Let him that hath understanding count the number of the beast: for it is the number of a man; and his number is Six hundred threescore and six.

3. Why does the Vatican own a telescope by the name of Lucifer located at the Mount Graham International Observatory Near Mount Graham, Arizona

Large Binocular Telescope

From Wikipedia, the free encyclopedia

'LUCIFER' redirects here. For other uses, see Lucifer (disambiguation).

The **Large Binocular Telescope** (LBT) is an optical telescope for astronomy located on 10,700-foot (3,300 m) Mount Graham, in the Pinaleno Mountains of southeastern Arizona, United States. It is a part of the Mount Graham International Observatory. When using both 8.4 m (330 inch) wide mirrors, with centres 14.4 m apart, the LBT has the same light-gathering ability as a 11.8 m (464 inch) wide single circular telescope and the resolution of a 22.8 m (897 inch) wide one.

The LBT mirrors individually are the joint second-largest optical telescopes in continental North America, next to the Hobby–Eberly Telescopes in West Texas. It has the largest monolithic, or non-segmented, mirror in an optical telescope.

https://en.wikipedia.org/wiki/Large_Binocular_Telescope

Why was the Pope's audience hall designed to look like a snake head?

*https://www.google.com/
search?q=pope+snake+build-
ing&rlz=1C5CHFA_enUS842US842&sx-
srf=ALeKk028CUiDRIHNVCzde-
gWFdcRxyBIahQ:1621850215471&tb-
m=isch&source=iu&ictx=1&fir=Gq-*

zTNIrX3zadeM%252CzX3NbomdFydfqM%252C_&vet=1&usg=AI4_-kRMSeJw-
CGGR-9MdAxqnu2s9YkhXqQ&sa=X&ved=2ahUKEwiB6uLvhuLwAhWPHM-
oKHZanCWQQ9QF6BAgQEAE&biw=1292&bih=577#imgrc=GqzTNIrX3zadeM

4. Why would Jeffrey Epstien want to create his own race of people?

https://www.nytimes.com/2019/07/31/business/jeffrey-epstein-eugenics.html

5. Why would Bill Gates have Marina Abramovic as his spiritual advisor?

6. Why would Bill Gates feature Marina Abramovic in his Microsoft commercial that ran on Easter 2020?

7. Why would the Founder of Black Lives Matter admit to summoning up spirits?

https://www.youtube.com/watch?v=bc010-TKNlg

8. Why would the Founder of Black Lives Matter Patrice Cullers admit to being a trained marxists?
We are trained Marxists." – Black Lives Matter Founding Member – Patrisse Cullors

https://www.bitchute.com/video/wM7Lziw65yBP/

9. Why would anyone write the Rockefeller plan?

The Rockefeller Plan is being executed:

Scenarios for the Future of Technology and International Development

https://www.dropbox.com/s/njzljlhebyjnqbz/Rockefeller%20 Foundation%20%281%29.pdf?dl=0 (UPLOAD TO TIMETOFREEAMERICA.COM and USE THE URL)

10. Why would the National Institute of Health be developing a Superparamagnetic nanoparticle delivery of DNA vaccine technology?

Superparamagnetic nanoparticle delivery of DNA vaccine

https://pubmed.ncbi.nlm.nih.gov/24715289/

11. Why would Charles Schwab Write a Book called COVID-19: The Great Reset?

https://images-na.ssl-images-amazon.com/ images/I/41-L+UlJgYL._ SX322_BO1,204,203,200_.jpg

WHAT ARE RESOURCES THAT YOU CAN TRUST IN A WORLD OF CENSORSHIP, TECH TYRANNY AND CANCEL CULTURE?

PASTORS WHO ARE UNAPOLOGETICALLY SHARING THE GOSPEL, THE TRUTH AND THE IRREFUTABLE WORD OF GOD FOUND IN THE BIBLE:

⬦ **Global Vision Bible Church**

Pastor Gregg Locke

https://www.globalvisionbc.com/

⬦ **Godspeak Calvary Chapel**

Pastor Rob McCoy

https://godspeak.com/

⬦ **GUTS Church**

Pastor Bill Scheer

https://www.gutschurch.com/

◇ **HIS Church**
Pastor Brian Gibson
https://hischurch.cc/

◇ **Influence Church**
Pastor Phil Hotsenpiller

◇ JD Farag
https://www.jdfarag.org/

◇ **Sheridan Church –**
Pastor Jackson Lahmeyer
https://www.sheridan.church

◇ **Real Faith**
Pastor Mark Driscoll
https://realfaith.com/

◇ **The Remnant Church**
Pastor Leon and Maria Benjamin
https://rumble.com/vgxhil-the-remnant-church-with-pastor-leon-benjamin-week-1.html

DOCTORS YOUR FAMILY CAN TRUST AND THAT YOU TRUST TO TREAT YOU IF YOU CONTRACT COVID-19

◇ 250+ Doctors in All 50 States Willing to Treat COVID-19 Patients with Affordable, Effective Proven Therapies and Treatments
www.AAPSOnline.org

◇ <u>Drs. Mark and Michele Sherwood</u> are the founders of a successful medical practice that has helped thousands of COVID-19 patients with 0 deaths.
www.Sherwood.TV

◊ Dr. Jim Meehan
   COVID Treatment and Prevention
   MeehanMD.com

◊ Dr. Richard Bartlett and a
   network out doctors in all 50 states are willing to
   provide you effective COVID-19 treatments and
   therapies
   BudesonideWorks.com

◊ Doctor Simone Gold has assembled an incredible
   team of Doctors in all 50 states who are successfully
   treating COVID-19 patients.
   https://www.americasfrontlinedoctors.com

EMAIL PROVIDERS THAT YOU CAN TRUST

◊ **Email:**
   www.ProtonMail.com

◊ Mass Blast Email Platform
   https://www.arialsoftware.com/

INTERNET BROWSERS YOU CAN TRUST

◊ Brave

INVESTMENTS TO PROTECT YOUR WEALTH AGAINST INFLATION

◊ Gold and Silver

◊ Andrew Sorchini - 310-433-3524
   www.BH-PM.com

◊ Kirk Elliott

   https://sovereignadvisors.net

◊ *www.TreasureIslandCoins.com*

◊ *https://www.stevequayle.com/*

◊ *https://schiffgold.com/*

◊ Silver – Andrew Sorchini – 310-433-3524

TRUSTWORTHY LAWYERS WILLING TO FIGHT BACK YOU CAN TRUST

◊ Attorney Leigh Dundas
   www.LeighDundas.com

◊ Attroney Thomas Renz
   https://www.OhioStandsUp.org/

◊ Legal/Legal-Eagle-Dream-Team
   https://www.AmericasFrontlineDoctors.org/

◊ America's Frontline Doctors
   https://www.americasfrontlinedoctors.com/

◊ Defending the Republic
   https://DefendingTheRepublic.org/

MEDIA THAT YOU CAN TRUST

◊ *American Thinker*
   https://www.americanthinker.com/

◊ *Breitbart News Network*
   https://www.breitbart.com/

⬦ *Censored News*
  www.Censored.News

⬦ *Epoch Times*
  https://www.theepochtimes.com/

⬦ *The Gateway Pundit*
  https://www.thegatewaypundit.com/

⬦ *Human Events*
  https://humanevents.com/

⬦ *National File*
  https://nationalfile.com/

⬦ *Populist*
  https://populist.press/

⬦ *Red State*
  https://redstate.com/

⬦ *Undercover DC*
  https://uncoverdc.com/

⬦ *Washington Times*
  ttps://www.washingtontimes.com/

PAYMENT PROCESSORS YOU CAN TRUST

⬦ John Chambers
  American Payment Processor

⬦ Nick Logan
  Cornerstone Credit Card Processing
  https://cornerstonepaymentsystems.com/

◇ Payment Processing –
   www.FreeSpeechMerchants.com

PHONE SERVICE:

◇ Satellite phones allow you to place
   secure phone calls.
   www.SatellitePhoneStore.com

PODCASTS

◇ Absolute Proof
   https://michaeljlindell.com/

◇ BardsFM – Watch
   https://www.bards.fm/

◇ Conservatives on Telegram
   https://www.conservativesontelegram.com/

◇ The Dan Bongino Show
   https://rumble.com/c/Bongino

◇ Doug Billings Right Side Media
   https://dougbillings.us/

◇ Eric Metaxas
   https://ericmetaxas.com/

◇ Health Ranger Report
   Watch: *ttps://www.brighteon.com/channels/hrreport*

◇ *https://naturalnews.com/*

◇ Monkey Werx US
   https://www.youtube.com/channel/
   UCUmvAVqbS-_5feqZPHA99Lw

◇ Patriot Street Fighter

Scott McKay
   - https://rumble.com/c/PatriotStreetfighter
   - https://scottmckay.us/

◇ The Pete Santilli Show
   https://thepetesantillishow.com/

◇ Steel Truth

Ann Vandersteel
   https://www.steeltruth.com/

◇ The Thrivetime Show
   - https://rumble.com/c/ThrivetimeShow
   - https://www.thrivetimeshow.com/

◇ X22 Report- Watch
   - https://rumble.com/vcmywr-ep.-2374b-message-received-blackout-hello-george-time-to-show-the-world-the.html
   - https://x22report.com/

SEARCH ENGINE PLATFORMS YOU CAN TRUST

◇ Duck Duck Go
   https://duckduckgo.com/

SOCIAL NETWORK

◇ Clout Hub
   https://app.clouthub.com/forum

◇ Frank – The Voice of Free Speech
   Mike Lindell – *https://frankspeech.com/*

◇ Pure Social Network
   https://puresocial.tv/

◇ Rumble
   https://rumble.com/

◇ Telegram App

VIDEO PLATFORM

◇ Pure Social Network
   https://puresocial.tv/

◇ Rumble
   https://rumble.com/

◇ Brighteon
   https://www.brighteon.com/

VACCINE EXEMPTIONS YOU CAN TRUST / HOW TO GET THE VACCINE EXEMPTION

◇ religious-exemptions

WEB HOSTING YOU CAN TRUST

◇ Cloud Hosting
   www.MoJoHost.com

◇ Content Delivery Network
   www.HighWinds.com

WANT TO KNOW EVEN MORE?

Check out all of Clay's books

START HERE
The World's Best Business Growth & Consulting Book: Business Growth Strategies from the World's Best Business Coach.

DON'T LET YOUR EMPLOYEES HOLD YOU HOSTAGE
This candid book shares how to avoid being held hostage by employees.

THE ENTREPRENEUR'S DRAGON ENERGY
The Mindset Kanye, Trump and You Need to Succeed.

SALES DOMINATION
Clay Clark is a master of selling and now he wants to teach you his proven processes, scalable systems and sales mastery moves in a humorous and practical way.

BOOM
The 14 Proven Steps to Business Success.

THE ART OF GETTING THINGS DONE
Clay Clark breaks down the proven, time-tested and time freedom creating super moves that you can use to create both the time freedom and financial freedom that most people only dream about.

THRIVE
How to Take Control of Your Destiny and Move Beyond Surviving... Now!

SEARCH ENGINE DOMINATION
Learn the Proven System We've Used to Earn Millions.

WHEEL OF WEALTH
An Entrepreneur's Action Guide.

JACKASSARY
Jackassery will serve as a beacon of light for other entrepreneurs that are looking to avoid troublesome employees and difficult situations. This is real. This is raw. This is unfiltered entrepreneurship.

MAKE YOUR LIFE EPIC
Clay shares his journey and struggle from the dorm room to the board room during his raw and action-packed story of how he built DJConnection.com.

PODCAST DOMINATION 101
This book will show you how to prepare, record, launch, and begin generating income from your podcast, all from your home studio!

F6 JOURNAL
Meta Thrive Time
Journal.

TRADE-UPS
Learn how to design and
live the life you love,
how to find and create
the time needed to get
things done in a world
filled with endless digital
distractions, and more!

HOW TO REPEL
FRIENDS AND
NOT INFLUENCE
PEOPLE
The epic whale of a
tale featuring America's
self proclaimed most
humble male.

IT'S NOT LONELY
AT THE TOP
15 Keys to achieving a
successful, peaceful, and
drama-free life.
(3/4 of this book is
handwritten by
Clay Clark, himself).

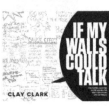

IF MY WALLS
COULD TALK
The Notes, Quotes, &
Epiphanies Written On
Clay's Office Walls.
(Hardcover).

CPSIA information can be obtained
at www.ICGtesting.com
Printed in the USA
LVHW031208271121
704585LV00006B/6